CONTENTS

Frightening Light

Introduction	7
Seeing the light	10
Horribly bright scientists	24
Bulging eyeballs	44
Sizzling sunshine	58
Frightening lighting	75
Frightening reflections	92
Frightening light-benders	109
Crucial colours	124
Blistering lasers	142
A brighter future?	154
Frightening Light quiz	159
Horrible index	169

CONTENTS

Sounds Dreadful

Introduction	177
Sounding off	180
Dreadful hearing	193
Speedy sound waves	212
Shattering sounds	232
Noisy nature	241
Eerie echoes	250
Dreadful body sounds	264
Dreadful musical mayhem	286
Dreadful sound effects	305
Rotten recordings	316
Sounding it out	328
Sounds Dreadful quiz	333
Horrible index	344

YO! A SCIENCE BOOK! **SOUNDS DREADFUL?** SOUNDS COOL TO ME, MAN!

FRIGHTENING LiGHT

INTRODUCTION

Science is frightening. Frighteningly confusing.

Take the topic of light. You see light every day in sunshine and light bulbs so you might think that the science of light would be light work.

But you'd be wrong. It's hard. Harder to crack than a dried pea from last term's school dinner. And as for the facts – they're harder to untangle than a vat of spaghetti.

See what I mean? Light = instant confusion! It's frightening. And if you ask a scientist to explain about light it's even worse. You're bound to get a long incomprehensible answer with lots of frighteningly complicated scientific words…

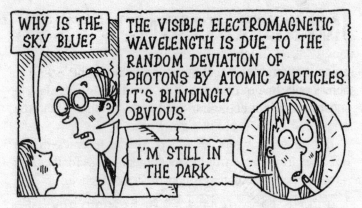

Horrible, isn't it? Yep – it's not surprising that Science can make your flesh creep.

Well, now to look on the bright side – here's a little light relief for you. Simply take this book to a quiet place, sit down and turn the pages. It will shed light on light science, and there are lots of light-hearted facts about eyeballs and laser surgery and ghostly lights and other dark and horrible corners of science. These could really brighten your day – especially when you frighten your teacher with a few tricky questions…

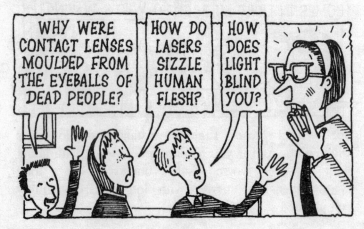

Your new-found knowledge of light science is sure to put your teacher in the shade. And afterwards, who knows? You might even become a leading light in science – then you'll really enjoy the limelight! So now there's only one question…

Are you bright enough to read on?

SEEING THE LIGHT

The sun was sinking behind the Brocken Mountain. The sky was getting darker by the minute and already the climber could scarcely see the narrow twisting goat-path at his feet. The climber was beginning to feel very afraid.

"It's time," he thought. "I'm going to see it any minute," and he peered anxiously at his pocket watch.

"Pull yourself together!" he said to himself. "You're a scientist. There must be a rational explanation. There's no such thing as ghosts."

But he trembled and his mouth felt dry as he wondered for the first time how he would find his way down in the dark. A bead of cold sweat trickled down his neck.

Suddenly his heart started thudding. Tiny hairs prickled on the back of his neck.

Somehow he knew even without a backward glance that he was not alone. There was someone ... or something on the mountain behind him. He tried to turn his head but his neck had locked rigid. At last he forced his whole body to swing round. His jaw dropped open in horror. Behind him, etched on the foggy clouds was a huge dark figure. Rings of ghostly light played around the terrifying outline as it hung in thin air.

The thing seemed to be watching him. Waiting. Waiting to pounce.

For a moment the climber seemed hypnotized. Then he forced himself to react. With trembling hands he pulled out a pocket book and a chewed stub of pencil. And started scribbling unreadable notes. All the time he was mumbling desperately.

"Fascinating phenomenon," he said, over and over again. "Fascinating. I – er – better get moving."

As the climber turned and scurried up the path the giant figure seemed to spring into life. It began climbing silently and effortlessly in the climber's footsteps. And whatever it was, it was coming after him, silently – faster and faster.

And reaching out its long shadowy arms…

DON'T PANIC! As the scientist realized, the figure was only his own shadow. This very real if ghostly effect is called the spectre of the Brocken after the Brocken Mountain in Germany where it's often seen. If you climb a mountain near sunset (not a very safe thing to do – so don't try it on your own) the low sun can cast your shadow on nearby clouds. And you see a huge ghostly figure. But this is just one of many horribly amazing light effects.

Read on for the frightening facts…

Frightening light fact file

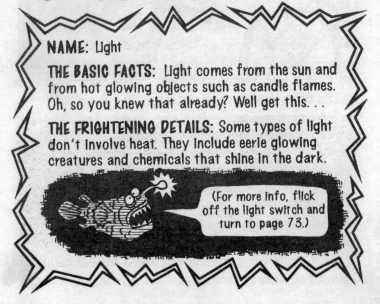

NAME: Light

THE BASIC FACTS: Light comes from the sun and from hot glowing objects such as candle flames. Oh, so you knew that already? Well get this. . .

THE FRIGHTENING DETAILS: Some types of light don't involve heat. They include eerie glowing creatures and chemicals that shine in the dark.

(For more info, flick off the light switch and turn to page 73.)

A GLOOMY THOUGHT

So you really did switch out the lights just then? Well, put them back on and read this.

It's easy to make light appear and disappear, isn't it? Every morning light appears in the sky and you don't even have to get out of bed to make it happen. So maybe that's why people take light for granted. And think it's no big deal.

Well, it is.

Imagine the sun doesn't rise tomorrow. Then imagine that all the light bulbs in the world go *phfutt* at the same instant.

And imagine also that even the distant stars fail to shine. The world would be very cold and very dark. And frightening and dangerous. Without light to see by, people would be bumping into each other and treading on the cat and knocking over priceless ornaments and skidding on banana skins.

And that's not all. Can you work out which other things you need light for?

13

FRIGHTENING LIGHT QUIZ

Without sunlight you can't see...
1 A rainbow. TRUE/FALSE
2 The moon. TRUE/FALSE

If it's completely dark...
3 Your face wouldn't appear in a mirror. TRUE/FALSE

4 You couldn't take holiday snaps. TRUE/FALSE
5 A poisonous rattlesnake couldn't find where you are hiding. TRUE/FALSE

1 TRUE. A rainbow happens when sunlight shines through droplets of rain. This splits the sunlight into different colours. (Check out pages 28-32 for the colourful details.) You actually get rainbows at night made by moonlight but the colours are too dim for your eyes to make out.

2 TRUE. The moon doesn't make its own light. That pretty silvery moonlight is actually sunlight that's bounced off (or as a scientist might say, reflected from) the moon. The surface of the moon is made of rock and dust but if it was ice it would reflect light really well and the moon would be nearly as bright as the sun.

3 TRUE. A mirror works by reflecting light. There's nothing to stop you looking at the bathroom mirror in the dark. But since there's no light the mirror won't reflect your image. Mind you, according to legend, if you're a vampire the mirror won't show your image anyway.

4 TRUE. Imagine you went pot-holing in a dark cave and left your torch at home. Whoops. You couldn't take any snaps because the chemicals that make a photograph only work if light falls on the film.

5 FALSE. The rattlesnake has a pit on each side of its head full of temperature sensors. These detect heat from your body. It's frightening. And that's why hiding from the snake in a dark cupboard isn't such a clever idea.

15

THE LIGHT FANTASTIC

So light brightens up your life, but take a closer look at light and it becomes even more fantastic... Imagine you could look at a ray of light through an incredibly powerful microscope. It would have to be billions of times more powerful than the world's most powerful microscope. Here's what you might see.

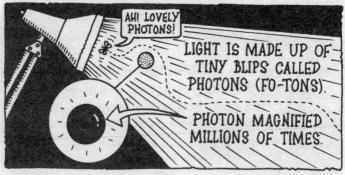

Photons are never still – they whiz along in the form of light waves. And hundreds of light waves could stretch across this full stop.

Photons sound phenomenal, don't they? You can imagine them as tiny little super-heroes flying through the air

16

with awesome powers – so here's a story about one of them. Ooops – before you read it, I ought to tell you that an atom is a tiny ball of matter. Everything in the known universe – including you and me and this book – are made of different combinations of different types of atom.

THE ADVENTURES OF SUPER-PHOTON

IS IT A BIRD? IS IT A PLANE? NO, IT'S SUPER-PHOTON!

The story so far...

HI!

Super-Photon was born deep inside the sun. He leapt fully formed from a super-heated atom.

But he has awesome superhuman energy. He flies in a light wave that wiggles to and fro 600,000,000,000,000 (that's six hundred trillion) times per second to form a light wave. And he never runs out of puff.

Continued overleaf...

ZERO! Super-Photon weighs nothing at all. He's far too small to see, far smaller even than an atom.

But the most incredible thing about Super-Photon isn't his super-hero powers – it's the fact that he's *nothing special*. You make photons all the times by zapping atoms with energy – for example by heating. That's why the toaster element glowed red when you burnt the toast this morning and that's why bulbs glow when you switch on the light. What happens is the cloud of electrons that whiz around the centre of an atom spit out photons in the form of light waves.

Each light wave is actually made up of a linked electric and a magnetic wave moving in the same direction. And since you can't get one without the other scientists lump them together and say that a light wave is a form of electromagnetic wave.

Bet you never knew!

1 The more energy you blast an atom with the more times the light wave will wiggle per second. And if you want to sound like a scientist you say "I am increasing the frequency of the electromagnetic waves".

2 At lower levels of energy you make radio waves, but turn up the power and you'll make different colours of light (from red going up to violet). Turn it up a bit more and you make ultraviolet light – a kind of high-energy light that you can't see. Keep going to maximum levels and you blast out deadly gamma rays.

3 You might wonder what happens to photons after they hit something. Well, remember a photon is just a blip of energy. It hits an atom and its energy is soaked up. So it's bye-bye photon. But photons do much more than whiz around...

Dare you discover … what light can do?

To begin with:

Wrap some kitchen foil round the end of a small bright torch.

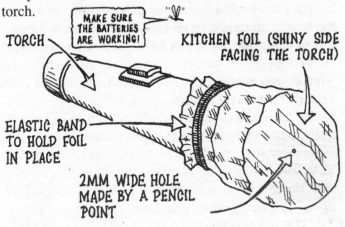

MAKE SURE THE BATTERIES ARE WORKING!

TORCH

KITCHEN FOIL (SHINY SIDE FACING THE TORCH)

ELASTIC BAND TO HOLD FOIL IN PLACE

2MM WIDE HOLE MADE BY A PENCIL POINT

You will need:

YOUR TORCH PREPARED AS SHOWN

ERK! IT'S MILKY AND MURKY!

A SQUARE BOTTLE OR STORAGE JAR WITH 9CM OF WATER. ADD A DROP OF MILK IN WITH THE WATER AND STIR. THE WATER SHOULD BE VERY SLIGHTLY CLOUDY, BUT STILL SEE-THROUGH.

9CM

Experiment 1:

1 Place the jar in front of a dark object. A dark book or some gloomy wallpaper will do.

2 Put your torch up the sides of the jar and switch on the light. You should be able to see the beam of light.

3 Now shine the light up so it hits the underside of the water.

What do you notice?

a) The light seems to flicker like a dodgy TV.

b) The light dances sideways.

c) The light seems to bounce down at an angle.

Experiment 2:

Now place the torch about 5 cm away from the sides of the jar. Try shining the light up or down from different angles.

What do you notice?

a) From some angles the light beam suddenly jumps to one side as it passes through the sides of the jar.

b) The water begins to heat up and bubble as you move the light.

c) No matter how you move the torch the light beam is always a straight line.

Answers:

1 c) The light bounces (reflects) off the underside of the water. The surface of the water is very smooth and the photons of light can all reflect in the same direction.

2 a) Light doesn't always go in a straight line. When light travels from air to water it slows to 224,900 km per second. This is because the photons have to push through lots of atoms in the water – just imagine a crowd of people trying to run.

---

through another crowd. When a beam of light hits the water at an angle one side of the beam slows before the other. This makes the beam bend.

FRIGHTENING EXPRESSIONS

One astronomer says to another...

Is this refraction something to do with a football match?

Answer:
No. Scientists call the bending of light refraction (re-frak-tion).

By now you'll have realized...
1 There's more to light than meets the eye.
2 That light is horribly amazing.
But you might also feel puzzled. If photons are so tiny and so fast how come scientists know so much about them? I mean, you can't exactly catch photons in a butterfly net. Well, it took the combined brain power of some frighteningly bright scientists to discover the truth.

TURN THE PAGE AND DISCOVER HOW THEY DID IT...

HORRIBLY BRIGHT SCIENTISTS

Much of our knowledge of light is based on the work of two scientific geniuses, Isaac Newton (1642–1727) and Albert Einstein (1879–1955). However, lots of scientists lent a hand. Well, as they say "many hands make LIGHT work", ha ha. Here's a handy spotter's guide to scientists who study light.

Spot the scientist

1. Physicists (Fizzy-cists)

INTERESTED IN: physical forces that shape the world – stuff like heat or electricity. The actual type of physicist featured in this book is an optical physicist. And – you guessed it – they study light.

WHAT THEY DO: set up experiments, make calculations about the speed of light and other exciting topics.

WHERE THEY WORK: university laboratories.

SPOTTER'S NOTE: physicists can be rather scruffy and absent-minded about their clothes. This is because they're too busy thinking about complex experiments to worry about how they look.

THOUGHTS ABOUT COMPLEX EXPERIMENTS

2. Astronomers

INTERESTED IN: stars and planets and other things you find in outer space. Astronomers are interested in light because we can only see space objects because of the light they produce or reflect.

WHAT THEY DO: scan the night sky using telescopes.

WHERE THEY WORK: observatories.

SPOTTER'S NOTE: astronomers are shy creatures that hide away in remote mountain-top observatories – but you can spot them in science conferences

CLOSE-UP OF RARE PHOTO SHOWING ASTRONOMER CREEPING OUT TO HER OBSERVATORY AT NIGHT

3. Ophthalmologists (op-thal-mol-ogists)

INTERESTED IN: eyeballs, their diseases and how they work.

WHAT THEY DO: they're trained doctors who treat patients with eye problems. Some are surgeons who perform operations on the eye.

WHERE THEY WORK: hospital eye departments.

SPOTTER'S NOTE: it's hard to find an ophthalmologist because they're always busy. Loads of people have sight problems, you see?

HAVE YOU SEEN HIM YET?

IF I COULD SEE HIM I WOULDN'T BE HERE

OPHTH

25

PULLING A FAST ONE

For centuries scientists were keen to measure the speed of light. They knew that this would help them judge the distance of planets and so make more accurate astronomical observations. So loads of scientists had a go. But they had a problem. Light is kind of speedy. All light photons belt along at 299,792,458 metres a second. There's nothing faster in the known universe – not even kids leaving a science class on a Friday afternoon.

Now, you'd think it would be impossible to clock the speed of light. I mean, you'd need amazingly quick reactions and a very good stopwatch to do it – right? So how did scientists manage this impossible feat? First off the mark was Italian scientist Galileo Galilei (1564–1642).

GALLANT GALILEO

One dark night Galileo and a friend went into the mountains. Each man carried a lantern with a shutter.

Galileo climbed a hill. His friend climbed another hill three kilometres away. It was a cold, lonely and dangerous trek and if either man had fallen there was no hope of a quick rescue.

Once he reached the top of his hill Galileo opened the shutter of his lantern and started counting. The plan was for the friend to show his lantern in response to Galileo's signal.

To his relief Galileo saw the light from his friend's lantern and stopped counting.

COULD YOU BE A SCIENTIST?

But great Galileo was wrong – as he found out when he and his long-suffering pal tried climbing hills further apart. Light is so speedy that a few squitty kilometres make no obvious difference to the measurements. Galileo was simply timing how quickly he reacted to the light signals. He realised this and gave up.

LIGHT SPEED CLOCKED

Using complex calculations, astronomers were also trying to clock the speed of light. In 1676 Danish stargazer Ole Roemer (1644–1710) was watching Jupiter's moon Io when he figured out that the further away Earth was from Jupiter, the longer it took light to reach his telescope. Using Roemer's data, scientists reckoned that light travelled at about 225,000 km per second. Not bad – but not right. Then in 1725 British astronomer James Bradley came up with a new figure using brain-blistering sums such as the angle of his telescope and the speed of the Earth. He was just five per cent out.

Meanwhile, back in the hills. In 1849 French physicist Armand Fizeau (1819–1896) shone a bright light from the top of a hill. The light shone through the spokes of a spinning wheel and bounced off a mirror on a hilltop eight km distant before returning through the wheel.

I WORKED OUT THE SPEED OF LIGHT BY MEASURING THE DISTANCE THE WHEEL TRAVELLED, ITS SPEED AND THE DISTANCE LIGHT TRAVELLED

THAT'S 'WHEELY' CLEVER!

His figure of 313,300 km per second was a bit too speedy. But the technique proved to be a bright idea and was used by other scientists.

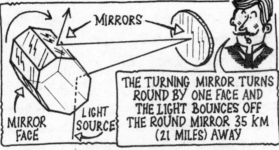
IZZY THE INCREDIBLE

One scientist played a key role in bringing the secrets of light to light – he was Isaac Newton. Of course, any old teacher will tell you that Newton is famous for describing the fatal forces that can affect a moving object – forces such as gravity. But do they also know that Newton's pet dog was named Diamond? Now Diamond wasn't quite as smart as his brainy owner. Here's what his diary might have looked like if he'd learnt to write.

A dog's diary
by Diamond

Cambridge ~ 2 June 1664

My master, Isaac is grumpy today. Oh well, so what — he's a miserable human. Mind you his bark is worse than his bite — ha ha. Actually, Isaac's mum is to blame. Isaac and I are at College but Isaac's skint. Isaac's mum is really rich but she never sends us any pocket money. So poor Isaac has to earn a few pennies by working as a waiter in the College. Then he's allowed to eat the scraps and leftovers. And guess what I get? Isaac's scraps and leftovers.

Oh well, it's a dog's life.

YUK!

31 August

Isaac is barking mad. (Well mad, anyway.) We went to a fair but instead of buying a nice juicy joint of meat for me, Isaac spent his hard-earned pennies on a prism. Well, he calls it a "prism". I call it a stupid triangular lump of glass that you can't even eat. So I whimpered in protest.

Isaac looked down at me in surprise.

"Are you OK?" he asked.

My master often talks to me because he doesn't have too many human friends.

"I'm rough," I replied.

Actually it sounded more like "ruff!" so Isaac ignored me. Well, he's still working and I'm dog-tired. So I'm taking my grumbling belly off to bed.

RUFF

Woolsthorpe, Lincolnshire ~ 25 December 1665

We're here staying with Isaac's mum. It's all to do with something called "the plague". Well, humans are dropping dead like flies and the College is closed. So we came here. It's a good thing this plague. Now I get fed regularly by Isaac's mum. Yum, yum – Christmas goose bones.

1 January 1666

My master missed supper ... again. As usual, he's up in his room scribbling masses of meaningless numbers and mumbling scientific gibberish about light. He never washes or changes his clothes – phwoar, he's really going to the dogs. Mind you, I'm always ready to help my master. That's why I made

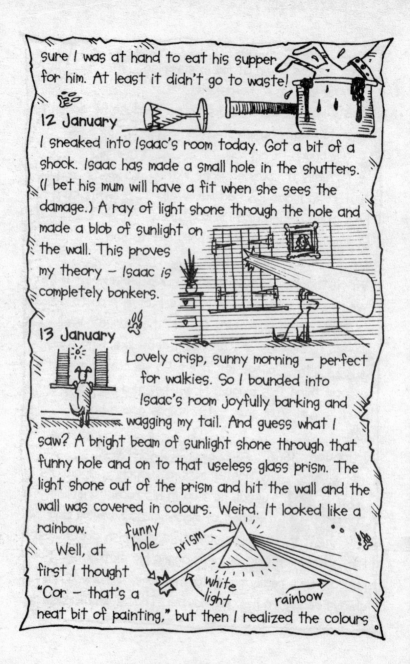

sure I was at hand to eat his supper for him. At least it didn't go to waste!

12 January

I sneaked into Isaac's room today. Got a bit of a shock. Isaac has made a small hole in the shutters. (I bet his mum will have a fit when she sees the damage.) A ray of light shone through the hole and made a blob of sunlight on the wall. This proves my theory — Isaac *is* completely bonkers.

13 January

Lovely crisp, sunny morning — perfect for walkies. So I bounded into Isaac's room joyfully barking and wagging my tail. And guess what I saw? A bright beam of sunlight shone through that funny hole and on to that useless glass prism. The light shone out of the prism and hit the wall and the wall was covered in colours. Weird. It looked like a rainbow.

Well, at first I thought "Cor — that's a neat bit of painting," but then I realized the colours

funny hole

prism

white light

rainbow

were made by the light. "Maybe that prism has magical powers," I thought.

Then I saw the broad grin on Isaac's face.

"What do you think of the rainbow, Diamond?" he whispered excitedly, pressing his face up close.

"Woof!" I replied. This is usually the best response when Isaac gets worked up about something.

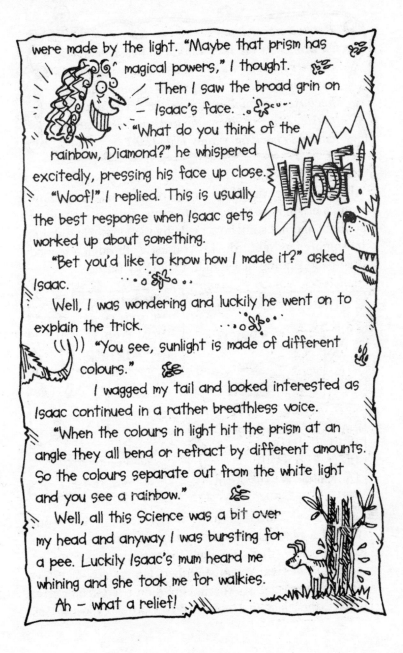

"Bet you'd like to know how I made it?" asked Isaac.

Well, I was wondering and luckily he went on to explain the trick.

"You see, sunlight is made of different colours."

I wagged my tail and looked interested as Isaac continued in a rather breathless voice.

"When the colours in light hit the prism at an angle they all bend or refract by different amounts. So the colours separate out from the white light and you see a rainbow."

Well, all this Science was a bit over my head and anyway I was bursting for a pee. Luckily Isaac's mum heard me whining and she took me for walkies.

Ah – what a relief!

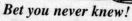
BLAZING A TRAIL

Although Isaac wasn't the first person to make a rainbow using a prism he was the first to prove colours are part of sunlight and not somehow made by the glass. He did this by shining red light from his "rainbow" through a second prism and finding that it didn't split any further.

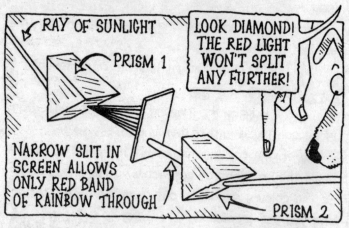

RAY OF SUNLIGHT

PRISM 1

LOOK DIAMOND! THE RED LIGHT WON'T SPLIT ANY FURTHER!

NARROW SLIT IN SCREEN ALLOWS ONLY RED BAND OF RAINBOW THROUGH

PRISM 2

Isaac had blazed a trail in Science but his work sparked a blazing row. He sent an account of it to the Royal Society (that's the club for top scientists founded in 1662) but rival scientist Robert Hooke (1635–1703) claimed that Isaac's experiments didn't work properly. In fact, the glass in Hooke's prism probably wasn't as clear as Newton's so he couldn't get the same results. But as a result of the row Newton stopped speaking to Hooke.

Isaac also suffered in another kind of blaze. He returned to Cambridge after the plague but one Sunday he went to church leaving a candle burning in his laboratory. Perhaps Diamond wanted to try a few experiments too. Anyway, he jumped on the table, knocked over the candle and started a fire. According to one report, the blaze destroyed all Isaac's notes on light and all his chemistry equipment. I expect poor Diamond ended up in the dog house.

Isaac rewrote his notes from memory. But he didn't publish any of his work until 1704. By this time Hooke was dead so Isaac got the last word on light. Except, of course, it wasn't the last word. Isaac had reckoned light was made of tiny balls. But there was no way he could see the balls so his idea is a bit of a stab in the dark – ha ha. And within a century a brilliant scientist would see the problem in a different light.

Hall of fame: Thomas Young (1773–1829)
Nationality: British

Young Tom Young was frighteningly clever. He was so brilliant at school that the whole class probably wanted to sit next to him in Science tests. He learnt to read when he was two. By the time he was six he'd read the Bible – twice. By the time he was 14 he was designing telescopes and microscopes with the help of a friendly teacher. By then he could speak four languages besides English and he decided (no doubt as a bit of light relief) to teach himself eight more.

I'LL LEARN RUSSIAN, POLISH AND CHINESE... THEN I'LL HAVE LUNCH

Tom trained as a doctor but in 1797 his uncle died and left him a fortune. This was good news. Well, not for the uncle, but good news for Tom. At last he could afford to do what he really wanted – lots of lovely science experiments.

Unfortunately few people got to hear of Tom's discoveries. His articles were so boring that not many people bothered to read them. Not surprising really – Tom was sacked from a job at the Royal Institution because his lectures were too dull. (Note: this is unlikely to happen to your teacher. So stop daydreaming and get on with this book.)

In 1803 Tom proved that light takes the form of light waves. This was quite an achievement because as you know light waves are too small to see – 14,000 light waves could stretch across your thumbnail. In fact, the idea of light waves wasn't totally new. It had been put forward in 1690 by Dutch astronomer Christiaan Huygens (1629-1695) who based his suggestion on complex maths. But it was Thomas Young who dreamt up the experiment that proved light waves really exist.

Here's how he did it...

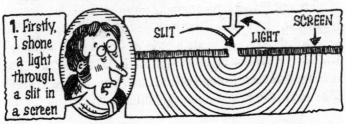

2. The light passed through two slits side by side in a second screen and spread out.

SECOND SCREEN WITH TWO SLITS

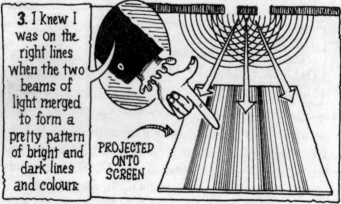

3. I knew I was on the right lines when the two beams of light merged to form a pretty pattern of bright and dark lines and colours.

PROJECTED ONTO SCREEN

4 Tom was able to show how this pattern was made by waves of light spreading out from the two slits. The two sets of waves spread out and passed through each other. Where the waves got in each other's way they made shadows – those were the dark lines.

Remember that light contains different colours? Where two light waves only partly blocked each other's way you saw the colours made by the waves that got through. But at the points the two sets of light waves actually managed to pass through one another you saw them both. This made the bright lines. Got all that?

FRIGHTENING EXPRESSIONS

One physicist says to another…

HOW'S YOUR DIFFRACTION?

I'M WORRIED ABOUT INTERFERENCE.

So who's interfering with the action?

Answer:
Hopefully, no one. **1.** Diffraction means light waves spreading out after passing through a narrow gap. **2.** Interference is a posh word for the effect that Young saw when two waves meet and either make a brighter light or colours or block one another out. (This effect turns up in the oddest places – keep an eye open for it in the rest of this book.)

THE FINAL, FINAL WORD?

More evidence built up to show that light took the form of waves and that Huygens and Young were right. For example, in 1818 French physicist Augustin Jean Fresnel (1788–1827) used brilliant maths to show how light waves can produce reflections and refraction. But was light really nothing more than a collection of waves? Was Newton's idea of light just a load of nonsense?

In 1901 German physicist Max Planck (1858–1947), spoilt the party. Planck said light is actually made of blips of energy called "quanta" (kwan-ta). Max's figures explained how the energy of light can be turned into heat inside a black box. But the only way his calculations added up was if light comes in quanta. These quanta are now called photons.

Four years later a scientific mega-genius used maths to prove Planck right. He performed no experiments and used only a pen and notepad for calculations. But he was able to prove that light was made up of photons, but that each blip moves so fast it forms a light wave. This idea was gradually accepted by physicists.

So who was this extraordinary scientist?

EXTRAORDINARY EINSTEIN

Albert Einstein is best known for his theories of relativity which he came up with in 1905 and 1915.

I HAVE PROVED THAT TIME AND SPACE ARE THE SAME THING AND THAT TIME CAN BE AFFECTED BY SPEED

If you haven't a clue what he's talking about, don't worry – you're not alone. There's a good chance that your teacher isn't aware of the finer details either.

BUT WHAT DOES HE MEAN, MISS?

ER, THAT'S ENOUGH SCIENCE FOR TODAY, ...GET YOUR READING BOOKS OUT

Of course, most well-informed teachers can tell you that Einstein was born in Germany, that he made his 1905 discoveries whilst working in Switzerland, and that from the 1930s he lived in America. But here's five facts they probably don't know about awesome Albert.

1 Einstein got interested in light at the age of 14 when he was daydreaming (no doubt during a particularly boring Science lesson). He imagined he was riding on top of a beam of light.

BEAM ME UP, SCOTTY!

This was dangerous (that's daydreaming, not riding on light – as you know, it's impossible to surf on light). In those days, the punishment for not paying attention was a whack across the knuckles with a cane. History doesn't record whether Albert suffered this punishment but he probably did.

2 Einstein was eventually expelled from school. His teacher couldn't stand the sight of him lolling at the back of the class and smiling and not doing any work. But Einstein was a genius and he was more interested in his own studies. (The chances are you won't get away with this excuse.)

IT'LL TAKE MORE THAN NOT COMBING YOUR HAIR TO MAKE YOU A GENIUS, JENKINS

3 Some people think that Einstein's discoveries about light were actually made by Mileva Einstein – Albert's first wife. Albert once remarked:

However their son, Hans Albert, explained that although Mileva helped with the maths it was Albert who did the scientific thinking. Albert probably meant that having Mileva to look after him gave him the time and confidence to develop his ideas.

4 After Einstein's death, a doctor removed the great man's brain, sliced it into little bits and stored it in a couple of large jars. His aim was to give it away to researchers into genius. At one point the doctor and reporter drove across the USA to present the sliced-up brain to Einstein's grand-daughter. But she didn't want the grily relic.

5 At the same time as his brain was taken, the doctor removed his eyeballs as souvenirs.

Would you want souvenirs like these? Probably not, and if squelching bloodshot eyeballs make you shudder you might want to close your own eyes before you turn the page.

Because the next chapter is *bulging* with them...

BULGING EYEBALLS

Here's a really FRIGHTENING thought. Imagine one morning you opened your eyes and saw nothing – just darkness. As black as the darkest night without even a glimmer of starlight. You'd be in a blind panic, wouldn't you? (Or you might think it actually was night and go back to sleep.)

 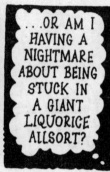 

Well, thank goodness for eyeballs. If it wasn't for them you wouldn't be able to see any light at all.

BULGING EYEBALLS QUIZ
If you're itching to know more about eyeballs, there's one opposite that's been freshly cut in half. In this quiz each part of the eyeball has a matching fact. All you have to do is match the bits of eyeball to the relevant facts...

EYEBALL BITS AND PIECES
1 Ciliary muscles
2 Iris
3 Optic nerve
4 Retina with rod and cone cells*

5 Cornea
6 Eyelashes
7 Lens
8 Watery bit
9 Sclera (sk-leer-a)
10 Eye muscles

*By the way the "cells" are more than 50 trillion tiny living jelly-like blobs that make up your body. But you probably knew that already.

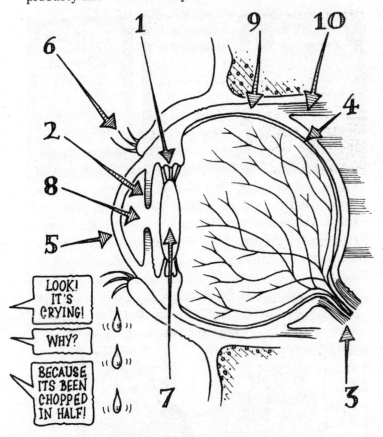

RELEVANT FACTS

a) There are 200 of these.

b) This bit helps to keep the eyeball in shape.

c) They stop your eyeball slopping out of its socket.

d) The colour of this bit stops light getting through and dazzling you.

e) This bit is 6.5 square cm. Without it you'd see nothing.

f) This bit changes shape 100,000 times a day.

g) This bit controls the eyeball part mentioned in **f)**.

h) This part sucks in oxygen gas from the air.

i) There are one million fibres in this bit.

j) You can see the blood vessels in this bit.

Answers:

1g) 2d) Light goes through the pupil – the hole in the middle. (The colour of your eye doesn't make any difference to what you see.) **3i)** They're nerve fibres. Their job is to take the pattern of light signals picked up by the retina to the brain in the form of nerve signals. **4e)** It's got 4.5 million cone cells to give you colour vision and about 90 million rod cells that detect light but not colours. (For more info. on colour vision see page 136.) **5h)** The cornea has no blood vessels to supply it with the sugar and oxygen it needs to stay alive. It gets sugars from the gloopy fluid in the eye and oxygen directly from the air. **6a)** They fall out after about three months, but you always grow more.

ERK! MY EYELIDS ARE GOING BALD!

7f) The lens thickens or lengthens so that light from whatever you are looking at is bent (refracted) and so focused on the retina. That's blinking amazing, isn't it? **8b)** Yes, it's true, you're looking at this page through a pool of watery jelly. **9j)** It's the "white" of your eyeball. When the eyeball is injured or has a disease the blood vessels get inflamed and get bigger. And the eyeball looks gungey and bloodshot. **10c)** They also swivel the eyeball round to look at things. Your brain coordinates the muscles on each eyeball so they work together. When this doesn't happen you go cross-eyed.

Bet you never knew!

1 The way your retina lets you see light is horribly complicated. When you look at something, photons of light hit the cells in the retina. These cells contain coloured chemicals called pigments. The photons spark a series of chemical reactions first in the pigments and then in the cells. These create a nerve signal that travels to the brain. And get this – all this confusing chaotic chemistry happens more or less instantly. And all the time.

2 So how good are your eyeballs? Are they sharp as needles or a sight for sore eyes? Why not put them through their paces? Your eyeballs should be good enough to spot a coin in the playground at 65 metres. Better make sure the playground is empty before trying this experiment, though.

Now for another eyeball test.

Dare you discover … how something horrible appears to happen to your hand?

You will need:

One red piece of A4 paper

One left hand (Go on use your own, it won't hurt … honest!)

What you do:

1 Roll the paper lengthways into a tube 2.5 cm across.
2 Stand with a window on your right.
3 Put the tube to your right eye. Stare hard with both eyes open.
4 Place your left hand against the left side of the tube with your thumb underneath the tube.

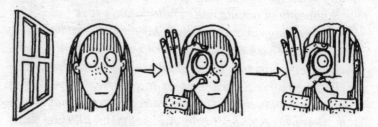

What do you notice?

a) Your hand … has disappeared.
b) Agggh! A bleeding hole has appeared in your hand.
c) Oh no! You've got two left hands.

Answer:
b) Your left and your right eyes are seeing different views. Your brain combines them to make a 3-D scene. This is what happens all the time when you look at things but in this case the scene is a rather horrible illusion.

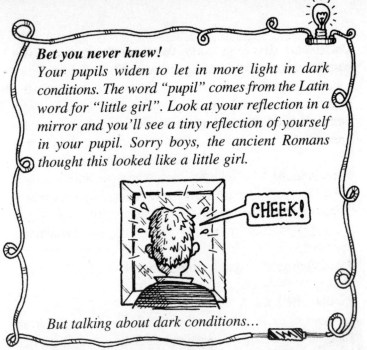

Bet you never knew!

Your pupils widen to let in more light in dark conditions. The word "pupil" comes from the Latin word for "little girl". Look at your reflection in a mirror and you'll see a tiny reflection of yourself in your pupil. Sorry boys, the ancient Romans thought this looked like a little girl.

CHEEK!

But talking about dark conditions...

TEACHER'S TEA-BREAK TEASER

This teaser works best in a dark, sinister, gloomy corridor (most schools have a few). You'll need a book with very small print. (Try using a boring science book, not this one, obviously.) Knock on the staffroom door. When the door opens smile sweetly and ask...

CAN YOU READ THIS FOR ME?

Enjoy watching your teacher struggling with the tiny print. Then ask them why people can't read in the dark.

Does your teacher know both answers?

COULD YOU BE A SCIENTIST?

Of course, these vital facts about vision didn't discover themselves. Scientists and doctors had to find them out by careful investigation. The discovery of how the lens in your eye focuses light was made by Thomas Young in 1792 using a real eyeball.

But where did it come from?

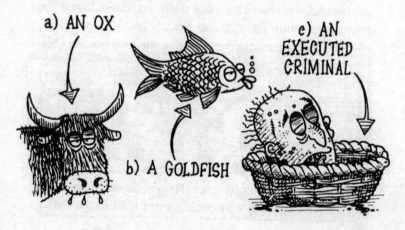

a) AN OX

b) A GOLDFISH

c) AN EXECUTED CRIMINAL

50

TEST YOUR TEACHER

You can liven up a boring swimming lesson by asking this tricky science question. It's sure to make a big splash.

*WHY DOES EVERYTHING APPEAR BLURRED UNDER WATER?

Answer:
Normally light refracts (that's bends, remember) as it passes through the cornea. This bending happens as light passes from the air into the watery cornea. This helps to bend light on to the retina allowing you to see things in focus.

51

When you're underwater the light is already going through water so it doesn't bend into the cornea. As a result the light isn't so well focused on your retina and things appear blurred.

HORRIBLE HEALTH WARNING!

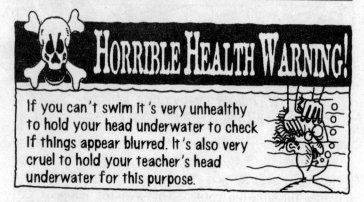

If you can't swim it's very unhealthy to hold your head underwater to check if things appear blurred. It's also very cruel to hold your teacher's head underwater for this purpose.

FRIGHTENING EXPRESSIONS

An ophthalmologist asks...

Talking about eye problems, take a very close look at this (if you can).

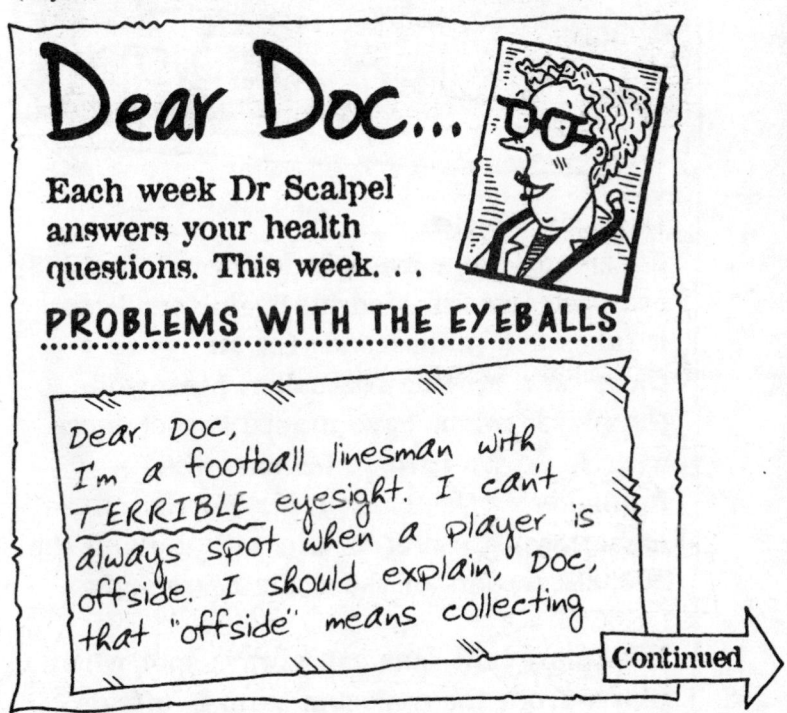

Dear Doc...

Each week Dr Scalpel answers your health questions. This week...

PROBLEMS WITH THE EYEBALLS

Dear Doc,
I'm a football linesman with TERRIBLE eyesight. I can't always spot when a player is offside. I should explain, Doc, that "offside" means collecting

Continued →

53

a forward pass with no opponents between you and the goal line when the ball is kicked. And it's not allowed. But as I said, I'm not always sure when a player is offside. You see, they move so fast it's very confusing. And when I make the wrong decision the fans call me rude names. It's so hurtful ... I could cry.
Should I retire?

Mr I.B. Worried

Dear Mr Worried
Cheer up – your eyesight is normal. In 1998 eye specialists in Madrid, Spain found that it takes 300 milliseconds for an eye to focus on a moving footballer. Meanwhile the player might have moved two or more metres. So it's hard to be sure when a footballer's offside. Well, Mr Worried, this embarrassing secret is safe with me and the 200,000 readers of the *Daily Searchlight*.

PS Funny how fans can always spot when a player from the opposing team is offside.

Dear Doc
I keep seeing dark dots in front of my eyes – am I going dotty?
I.C. Spottes

Dear Mr Spottes
The dots you describe are probably caused by blood clots on your retina. A larger dark spot may be caused by damage to your retina. In both cases you should see a doctor. I'm sure they'll spot the problem.

Dear Doc
My eyesight is gradually disappearing round the edges of my field of vision. When I look at a light I see a blurred halo around it. "Halo, halo, halo," I said to myself – I must be seeing things. What do you think?

Mrs N.O. Dark

Dear Mrs Dark

You sound like you might have glaucoma (gly-comb-a). The watery gloop in your eyeball is produced behind your iris. For reasons we doctors don't understand, you can make too much gloop. It builds up inside your eyeball pressing outwards until it squeezes your optic nerve – that's the nerve that takes signals from your retina to your brain. This reduces vision and causes blindness. But don't panic! You can take drops to cut the amount of gloop your eye makes and relieve the pressure on your nerve.

That's a relief – eh?

Dear Doc
Please help me – I think I'm going blind. My eyesight is blurred and dim. I keep seeing double. What's happening to me?

Ms Rabble

Dear Ms Rabble

You could have a cataract. A build up of fluid in the lens leads to chemical changes that cause a cloudy area. Seeing double happens when two cloudy areas refract light from the same object. Fortunately the cataract can be removed in a simple operation.

PS One traditional remedy for cataracts was to plop a warm drop of pee (or urine, as we doctors call it) into the eye. Don't try this – it's useless and may cause infection.

DON'T MISS NEXT WEEK. It 'snot' much fun having problems with your nostrils.
Dear Doc looks into noses...

There's lots of possible causes for cataracts, including damage to the lens after being outside too much under the huge sizzling blinding solar nuclear explosion in the sky.

The what?

The sun, of course.

It's time to put on those shades and turn the page...

SIZZLING SUNSHINE

We're all lucky people. Every day we get hours and hours of free sunshine. Well, OK, that's true for California and it's not quite so true if you're snowed up in Siberia. But even when the weather's grotty – cheer up – the sun's shining up there above the clouds providing warmth and light. And all for free!

But the sun is more than a big light bulb in the sky. The whole future of life on Earth depends on the sun. This fact is so basic even aliens know about it...

REPORT BY

Oddblob the Blurb

MISSION: Inter-planetary probe of medium-sized star system with a star known locally as the sun.

GALAXY CO-ORDINATES: 0001.1100.0011100.0

MAP:

ALIEN DRIBBLE

MARS

EARTH

VENUS

SUN

MERCURY

(SENSORS REVEAL AT LEAST FIVE OUTER PLANETS)

INTELLIGENT LIFE

A species known as humanoids are very abundant on Planet Earth. We have captured a specially trained humanoid known as a "Science teacher" for further research. The names given to planets in this report are names used by the humanoid.

Science teacher – emitted squeaky sound like, "ARR-YOR-AN-ALEEE-EN!"

STAR STATUS

The sun is in the middle of its life. It is 4.5 billion years old. The centre is 14,000,000° C (27,000,000° F). Light photons are produced by atoms as they are fused together. Just like any other star of this type, really.

PLANET EARTH

This planet is the only one suitable for life. Life on planet Earth depends on light from the sun.

PLANTS – GREEN NON-MOVING LIFE FORMS. PLANTS USE ENERGY FROM SUNLIGHT TO TURN WATER AND CARBON DIOXIDE GAS FROM AIR INTO FOOD.

SUN – ENERGY

HUMANOIDS EAT ANIMALS AND PLANTS.

ANIMALS – MOBILE LIFE FORMS THAT EAT PLANTS OR OTHER ANIMALS.

Sensors report that without the sun there would be no plants, no animals and humanoids would be missing out on their intake of nutritive chemicals otherwise known as lunch.

INVASION POTENTIAL ◀ • • • • • • • •

Planet Earth is suitable for invasion – but from our study of the Science teacher we have established that humans spend much of their time communicating boring information. Life on Earth may prove unbearably dull for higher forms of intelligence such as Blurbs. So we have erased the humanoid's memory of our visit and put him back where we found him.

ZONK!...now where was I...ah yes, your science homework, Smith...

AWESOME ECLIPSES

One dramatic effect of the sun is called an eclipse. This is caused by the moon getting in the way of the sun's light so that its shadow falls on the Earth.

Oh, so you knew that? Well, in the past many people didn't – so they made up stories and performed rituals to make sense of what was going on.

1 An eclipse can be frightening. If you don't know what's happening, it looks like the moon is swallowing the sun. According to ancient Greek writer Thucydides (460-400 BC) an eclipse halted a battle in Persia in the sixth century BC. The two armies drew back and agreed to go on with the battle after a month, when any bad magical effects had worn off.

2 In ancient China people thought a dragon was eating the sun and banged gongs or pans to scare the monster away.

3 The native peoples of North America fired flaming arrows at the sky in a bid to re-light the sun.

THIS IS AN 'ARROWING EXPERIENCE!

4 The Pampas tribes of South America believed the moon goddess was darkened in an eclipse with her own blood drawn by savage dogs. Of course, they were barking up the wrong tree.

5 Some Tartar tribes in Asia believed the sun and moon were swallowed up by a blood-sucking vampire from a distant star.

6 In many countries people thought (wrongly) that diseases spread during eclipses. The Yukon tribes of Alaska covered their pots and pans during eclipses for this reason. A terrible outbreak of 'flu that claimed thousands of victims in South America in 1918 was blamed by some on an eclipse.

Dare you discover ... how to observe an eclipse?

Eclipses of the sun are fairly rare. There are often less than five a year – so chances are, you won't be able to see one from your own backyard. To see one you might have to travel to far flung places like the North Pole. Well, when you get there, here's a way to watch the eclipse without hurting your eyes.

Note: If there aren't any eclipses coming up you can always use this method to look at the sun safely. You can try it at home in a shaft of bright sunlight.

You will need:
The sun (but of course!)
A large sheet of white paper and something to fix it to the wall with
A small mirror
Ruler
A piece of card
Scissors and sticky tape

What you do:
1 Cut a circle in the card 2.5 cm across.
2 Tape the card over the mirror and stick the paper on the wall in a dark shadowy corner.
3 Hold the mirror so that it reflects the sunlight from the circle onto the white paper. You'll see a nice image of the Sun that's safe to look at.

URGENT HORRIBLE HEALTH WARNING!

Staring at the sun is dangerous. Even a few moments of being blasted by the Sun's high-energy photons kills off cells in your retina and gazing at the Sun too long can cause cataracts and blindness. Any really bright light can be harmful Welders who don't use protective goggles get "arc eye" and go blind for a while – or even for ever. So you'd be blind stupid to risk it.

A SNAP DECISION
If you think the dangers of observing an eclipse sound

rather frightening, spare a thought for Warren de la Rue (1815–1889). In 1860 top astronomer Sir John Herschel (1792–1871) asked this intrepid British photographer to travel to Rivabellosa in Spain to photograph an eclipse and prove a scientific fact.

"So Warren got a nice sun tan and took a few holiday snaps. What's so risky about that?" I hear you ask.

Well, in 1860 cameras were in their infancy and travel was a bit more primitive. So this was quite an undertaking. Here's what Warren's letters home might have looked like…

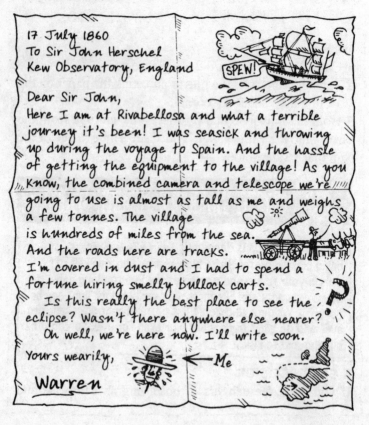

17 July 1860
To Sir John Herschel
Kew Observatory, England

SPEW!

Dear Sir John,
Here I am at Rivabellosa and what a terrible journey it's been! I was seasick and throwing up during the voyage to Spain. And the hassle of getting the equipment to the village! As you know, the combined camera and telescope we're going to use is almost as tall as me and weighs a few tonnes. The village is hundreds of miles from the sea. And the roads here are tracks. I'm covered in dust and I had to spend a fortune hiring smelly bullock carts.

Is this really the best place to see the eclipse? Wasn't there anywhere else nearer?

Oh well, we're here now. I'll write soon.

Yours wearily,

← Me

Warren

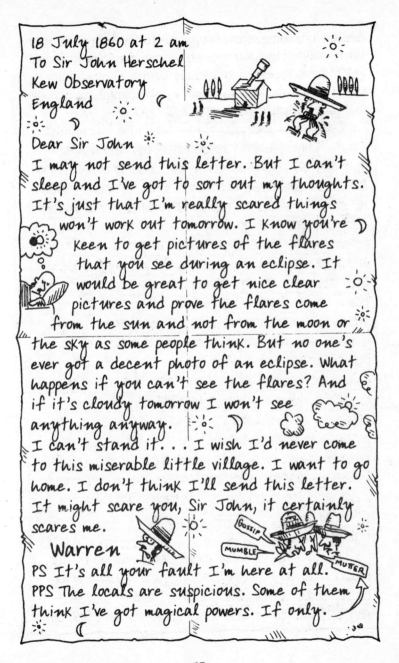

18 July 1860 at 2 am
To Sir John Herschel
Kew Observatory
England

Dear Sir John
I may not send this letter. But I can't sleep and I've got to sort out my thoughts. It's just that I'm really scared things won't work out tomorrow. I know you're keen to get pictures of the flares that you see during an eclipse. It would be great to get nice clear pictures and prove the flares come from the sun and not from the moon or the sky as some people think. But no one's ever got a decent photo of an eclipse. What happens if you can't see the flares? And if it's cloudy tomorrow I won't see anything anyway.
I can't stand it... I wish I'd never come to this miserable little village. I want to go home. I don't think I'll send this letter. It might scare you, Sir John, it certainly scares me.

Warren

PS It's all your fault I'm here at all.
PPS The locals are suspicious. Some of them think I've got magical powers. If only.

GOSSIP
MUMBLE
MUTTER

Meanwhile some of the people of Rivabellosa must have been wondering what was going on. Here's how events might have appeared to a young boy.

THE ECLIPSE BY PEDRO

Our teacher told us all about the eclipse. But the old people in our village said it would bring sickness and disaster. That's what Grandpa thought. He said the sweaty Englishman had a magic machine to make the sun go dark for as long as he wished.

The day of the eclipse was bright and sunny. I went up the hill with Grandpa to get a good view. Grandpa was still grumbling and saying no good will come of it. There were crowds of people. The Englishman had his machine set up — I could see the end of it sticking out the top of a shed like a giant gun.

Just before the eclipse, we saw the moon getting close to the sun. Then a horrible dark shadow appeared in the distance. It was the shadow of the moon. The darkness swept over the hills like a thunderstorm. Everything went grey. All the flowers closed up and birds started snoozing in the trees. It was just like evening so I started yawning.

"Bored already?" snapped Grandpa.

Then things got scary.   Grandpa

Little by little the sun was swallowed up by the moon until all you could see was a black glowing circle. Suddenly my hair stood on end — I was seriously worried. It was dark. The stars had come out.

Maybe Grandpa was right.

Perhaps the sun had gone for ever.

I grabbed hold of his hand.

Meanwhile the Englishman was acting crazy, shouting at his assistants and disappearing into the shed to work his giant machine. We heard him muttering things to himself.

"He's saying spells," whispered Grandpa.

So Grandpa got down on to his bony knees and started reciting prayers. But there was no sign of the sun.

Where was it?

The minutes dragged by...

Just then a bright bead of light appeared. It looked like a diamond ring around the dark moon. Everyone cheered. I found myself dancing up and down.

"It's a miracle!" cried Grandpa, struggling to his feet.

It began to get light. Soon the sun was shining again in the blue sky. The eclipse was scary but brilliant. No one got ill, nothing terrible happened. I wish we had an eclipse every week. It's much better than listening to Grandpa strumming his guitar and singing awful old songs.

18 July 1860 at 4 pm
To Sir John Herschel
Kew Observatory, England

Dear Sir John
It's over and I'm shattered. Completely drained. Well, I tried. I took 35 shots

67

including two when the sun was completely covered. But the pictures weren't as good as I'd expected. THEY WERE BETTER! LOADS BETTER! You can see everything. You can see the flares really clearly. It's blindingly obvious the flares are coming from the sun itself!!!

Thank you, Sir John, for sending me to this wonderful little village full of lovely people. Now for a giant party and everyone's invited!!

Love Warren xx
PS Wish you were here!

A scientist writes...

Spanish scientist Father Angelo Secchi (1818–1878) also took a series of photos of the eclipse. Father Secchi was over 400 km to the south-east but the flares in his pictures matched the ones taken by De La Rue. This was the final proof that the flares had definitely come from the sun.

DARK SECRETS

It gets dark during an eclipse because the moon casts its shadow over the Earth. You get a shadow any time a solid object blocks light. (That's how the climber on the Brocken Mountain made the "ghost".) Something that blocks light is described as opaque (o-payk). And you can use an opaque shape to make horrible shadows...

Dare you discover ... what lurks in the shadows?

You will need:
A pencil
A pair of scissors
A piece of black card. You can always paint a white piece of card black.
A piece of wire
Sticky tape
A small, bright torch
A room with light walls.

What you do:
1 Draw and cut out a monster shape.
2 Tape the wire to the bottom of the shape to make a handle.
3 Wait until it gets dark. Draw the curtains and switch on your torch. Place the torch about three metres from the wall.
4 Hold the wire so the shape is between the light and the wall. You can make brilliant sinister shadows. Hold on, sorry to spoil things, but this is a serious scientific experiment, after all. So...

What do you notice?

a) You moved the shape towards the wall and away from the torch. The shadow on the wall got larger.

b) When the shape is closer to the light it blocks more light. This throws a larger shadow on the wall.

c) As you moved the torch the shadow began to move in the opposite direction. Help – it's alive!

Answer:

b) When the shape is closer to the light, it blocks more light. This throws a larger shadow on the wall. The larger shadow has more of a blurred edge than the smaller one. This is because some light from the edges of the torch can still shine past the edges of the shape, but not enough to give a sharp edge to the shadow.

HORRIBLE HEALTH WARNING!

This monster shape is ideal for scaring your little brother or sister. But you know it's wrong – don't you? And you're going to resist the temptation, aren't you? Well ... aren't you?

STRANGE STARLIGHT

Of course, astronomers aren't just interested in sunlight. They're also very excited by the topic of starlight. If you have secret ambitions to be an astronomer you might like to train your telescope on this next bit...

The stars are a long way off. A very long way off. You'll remember that sunlight takes about eight and a half minutes to reach us. But that's a blink of an eye for starlight. Even the light of our next door neighbour star Alpha Centauri takes four years to arrive. But that's nothing. If you live in the northern part of the world the most distant object you'll see is the Andromeda galaxy. The photons from this star cluster set off 2.2 million years before you were born. And you thought waiting for the school bus took for ever.

Astronomers are interested in starlight because without it they wouldn't be able to see stars. And by studying the colour of the light they can work out the surface temperature of the star. For example, a bluish white star is a sizzling 27,760°C and a red star is a nice cool 2,000°C. (OK, that's cool by star standards – the hottest temperatures on Earth include California's Death Valley which reached 49°C in 1917. Any hotter than that here and it would be Death Valley for the human race.)

The brightness of a star can also be used mathematically to work out its distance. This brilliant fact was noted by U.S. astronomer Henrietta Leavitt (1868–1921).

Bet you never knew!
Stars are coloured. It's true! The reason they seem white to us is that most stars are very dim. They only give your eye about 500 photons a second. This means that we can only see them with our dim light detecting rod cells. And the rod cells can't see colours, can they?

COULD YOU BE AN ASTRONOMER?

You've probably heard the rhyme:

Twinkle, twinkle little star
How I wonder what you are!

72

Next time you gaze at a star consider this puzzle:

Why do stars twinkle?

a) Because their light flashes on and off.

b) Because the starlight is refracted (bent) by gusts of wind.

c) Because fast-moving clouds keep blocking the light.

Answer:
b) As the wind blows, the atoms that make up air may get more crowded together in one area than another. As light passes through this area it refracts (bends) producing a twinkling effect. In fact, moonlight does this too but because the moon appears bigger to us you don't notice it twinkling around the edges.

Bet you never knew!
If you want to spot stars it helps if you live a long way away from the neighbours. In built-up areas the night sky often glows with the light of streetlights and shop signs reflecting off water droplets and dust in the air. This spoils the view of the twinkling stars.

But if lights are bad news for astronomers they're very good news for small frightened kids who are scared of the dark. So if you're reading this at dusk, maybe you'd better turn on the light before you switch to the next chapter.

It will brighten you … and frighten you.

FRIGHTENING LIGHTING

This is a chapter about things that glow in the dark. And not all of them are light bulbs. Yep – long before anyone flicked a light switch, before even some bright spark invented fire, strange unearthly lights flickered in the darkness.

Intrigued? Let's bring the FRIGHTENING facts to light…

Frightening light fact file

NAME: Bioluminescence (bio-lum-min-nes-ance)

THE BASIC FACTS: 1. Certain living creatures can produce light.

2. Their bodies make a chemical called luciferin (loo-sif-fer-rin) and another called luciferase (loo-sif-fer-raze).

3. Luciferin combines with oxygen from the creature's blood and gives out light. Luciferase speeds up this chemical reaction.

THE FRIGHTENING DETAILS: Some bacteria do this. Some fish (see below) eat the bacteria. The bacteria remain alive and make light in the fish's skin.

'GLO' AWAY, YOU'RE UGLY!

THE GLOW IN THE DARK ZOO

Welcome to the world's first zoo where the animals provide the lighting...

Comb jelly

Jelly-fish-like creature 25-30cm long.

FOUND IN: Pacific and Atlantic Oceans.

LIGHT IS USED FOR: scaring off attackers.

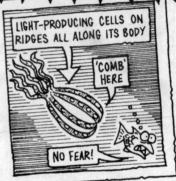

LIGHT-PRODUCING CELLS ON RIDGES ALL ALONG ITS BODY

'COMB' HERE

NO FEAR!

Deep sea angler fish

FOUND IN: deep oceans throughout the world

LIGHT IS USED FOR: catching other fish

WORM-LIKE BLOB (FILLED WITH GLOWING BACTERIA) ON THE END OF A LINE LURES SMALLER FISH TO THEIR DOOM.

HMMM, INTERESTING!

76

Fire flies and glow-worms

FOUND IN: fire flies live in North America and glow-worms live in Europe. Actually they're both varieties of beetle.

PHWOAR! HE'S NICE!

FIRE FLY

LIGHT IS USED FOR: signalling for a mate.

HERE I AM, BOYS!

Both insects have glowing lights on their bottoms. (Imagine you had one of these – you'd never need a rear bike light.)

GLOW-WORM

Luminous plankton

Tiny creatures often less than 1 mm long called copepods (cope-pods). The plankton also include plants called dinoflagellates (di-no- fladge- gell-ates).

FOUND IN: every ocean especially where the water is rich in minerals.

COPEPOD

DINOFLAGELLATE

LIGHT IS USED FOR: scaring away attackers. Ship toilets are often flushed with seawater – if the plankton are present they make your toilet glow in the dark. (Is this what they call a "flash in the pan"?)

ARGH! WEIRD WEE WEE!

But there are other kinds of light around and these are not made by animals. Not living ones, anyway.

COULD YOU BE A SCIENTIST?

It's 200 years ago. You're walking home and you bravely decide to take a short cut through the graveyard. It's very dark – you're scared … and suddenly you see an eerie glow. What's causing it?

a) It's a ghost. Yikes I'm out of here.

b) It's a mass of glow-worms feeding off rotting vegetation.

c) It's gases from a rotting body.

Answer:

c) Before new cemeteries were opened up in Victorian times many old churchyards became full up. Dead bodies were buried one on top of the other under a shallow layer of soil. Germs inside the rotting bodies made methane and phosphine (foz-feen) gas. As the gases reached the surface they often caught fire as a result of chemical reactions with oxygen in the air. The result was a pale blue glow that was called a will o' the wisp.

AWFUL ARTIFICIAL LIGHT

We take it for granted that by flicking a switch we can have light whenever we want. It's a part of every day life and without it you wouldn't be able to see this page, or even see to do homework (that would be tragic!). But just imagine you lived a few hundred years before there were light bulbs. Don't worry, you didn't have to use the glowing gas from a dead body. But the alternatives were almost as frightening.

Ye olde LIGHT UP YOUR LIFE

home shopping catalogue

ROMANTIC CANDLES

Why not light your home with a genuine olde worlde candle as used by people since ancient Egyptian times. Wow, what a dazzling choice!

NOW WE HAVE TO WAIT 3500 YEARS FOR SOMEONE TO INVENT MATCHES

CONTINUED...

Traditional tallow candle

▷ Made with boiled up fat from around the kidneys of a dead cow, sheep or horse.

WE'VE RUN OUT OF TALLOW CANDLES, WIFE

Heat from the flame melts the fat.

▷ Beeswax – the de-luxe alternative. Genuine waxy stuff squirted from the bodies of bees and built up to make chambers for their grubs to live in.

The flame burns the fat.

The wick sucks up the fat.

Modern paraffin candle

▷ Made from oil.

▷ Burns with a nice bright flame

SORRY MUM, IT'S MADE A MESS...

GRRR, I'LL GIVE YOU WAX!

THE AMAZING ARC-LIGHT

Invented by British scientist Sir Humphrey Davy (1778-1829) in 1808

WELL, CANDLES WENT OUT WITH THE ARK

▷ Electric current jumps across the gap between two carbon rods. (Make sure there's a constant gap between two carbon rods as the light burns otherwise the rods will melt or the light will fizzle out.)

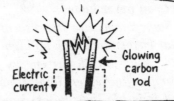

Electric current ▾

Glowing carbon rod

THE SMALL PRINT: This light is a fire hazard. And it could blind you because it's brighter than 4,000 candles. The only practical use anyone ever found for it was in the Dungeness lighthouse. So unless your house happens to be a lighthouse it's probably not such a good idea.

TURN IT OFF!

GASLIGHT

As invented by Scottish inventor William Murdock (1754–1839)

Flame made by burning coal gas

Handy tap to turn the gas on or off

ER – I'M JUST WARMING THE POT, MUM...

GRRR!

after an experiment in 1792 involving heating coal in his mum's teapot.

THE SMALL PRINT: You need pipes all over your house to carry the gas. And the gas is poisonous and can blow up your home. And even when it works the flame is smoky and smelly.

MARVELLOUS MODERN LIGHTS

Nowadays things are looking much brighter. Go into any street and you'll probably see sodium or mercury street lights. These work in roughly the same way.

An electric current passes through the tube. Atoms in the gas take in energy and give out light.

Something else passing through a tube

BRILLIANT BULBS

One invention put the others in the shade. The light bulb. And as every American knows the light bulb was invented by U.S. inventor Thomas A. Edison (1847–1931). And every well-informed Briton knows the light bulb was invented by British inventor Joseph Swan (1828–1914). So what's the truth?

Read on and find out…

Thomas A. Edison's diary

I've got this real smart idea for a new kind of light. All you do is send an electric current through a thin wire. This slows down the flow of electricity. The electric current drags along making the wire heat up and you get light. Simple but brilliant – like most of my inventions...

Hmm – need to pump out the air otherwise the thin wire will catch fire when you heat it up. You can't get fire without air – can you?

THIN WIRE

AIR IS MAKING THIN WIRE CATCH FIRE

ELECTRICITY

THE DAILY SUN

1 September 1878

Let there be light!

Brilliant inventor Thomas Edison is set to light up the world by inventing the light bulb. Already gas lighting company shares are plummeting at the prospect. And Edison hasn't even built a single bulb yet! But whiz-kid Edison is already famous for inventing the phonograph. (That's the new-fangled machine you can use to play music on.)

And now he's getting on with a bit of light work!

MR. T. EDISON

21 January 1879
If only I could make this light work. One day there could be a light bulb in every home. There might even be two in every

83

home. I could become seriously rich. But only if everything goes to plan. I've hurt my eyes staring at the light bulbs... before they burnt out. Work is getting harder.

Those carbon filaments sure can burn. Seems my pumps aren't good enough to get all the air out of the bulbs. So I tried platinum wires instead – but they kept melting. Then I made a switch to cut the power if the platinum gets too hot but the light keeps flickering. Oh well – back to the drawing board. As I like to say, "inventing is 99 per cent perspiration and only 1 per cent inspiration".

1 April 1879

Did I say perspiration? Well, I'm in a cold sweat just now. To be precise, I'm at my wit's end. We've tried thousands of materials – rubber, fishing line, wood and now in desperation we're trying human hair. Two of my assistants volunteered to provide the hair. John Kruesli's got a big bushy beard and J.V. Mackenzie's got wiry sideburns.

J.K.   J.V.M.

My staff are all excited and are even betting which hair will last longest without burning.

A few hours later...

Mackenzie's hair is still producing light! Hold on – looks like the electric current's been turned down and the bulb's too dim to be any use. RATS, I figure someone cheated to win the bets. I can't stand these failures – I should never have allowed the papers to print all that rubbish. Maybe I'll never solve this puzzle and go down in history as a dim failure.

17 October 1879

I was sitting in the office last night when a bright light bulb seemed to flash in my head. "Oh no – not another light bulb!" I moaned. Then I realized I was having A BRAINWAVE – that's what I mean by INSPIRATION. I thought burnt cotton thread that's turned to carbon might be the answer. Yeah – the magic material has to be carbon. After all, carbon only melts at really high temperatures of about 3500°C (6332°F). And now I've taken delivery of better air pumps the carbon shouldn't burn up. And ... well, I just have a hunch about cotton thread.

BUT WILL IT WORK?? ? ? ??

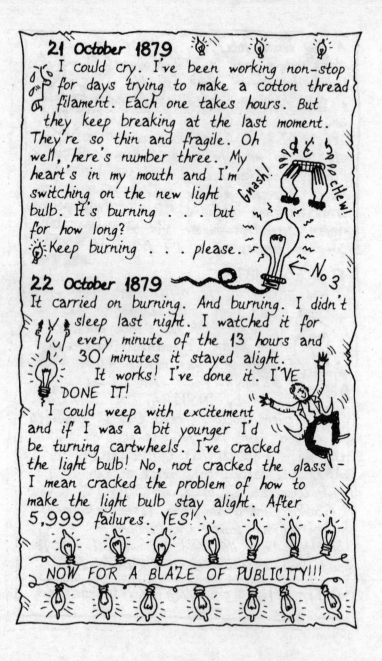

21 October 1879

I could cry. I've been working non-stop for days trying to make a cotton thread filament. Each one takes hours. But they keep breaking at the last moment. They're so thin and fragile. Oh well, here's number three. My heart's in my mouth and I'm switching on the new light bulb. It's burning . . . but for how long?

Keep burning . . . . please.

No 3

22 October 1879

It carried on burning. And burning. I didn't sleep last night. I watched it for every minute of the 13 hours and 30 minutes it stayed alight.

It works! I've done it. I'VE DONE IT!

I could weep with excitement and if I was a bit younger I'd be turning cartwheels. I've cracked the light bulb! No, not cracked the glass - I mean cracked the problem of how to make the light bulb stay alight. After 5,999 failures. YES!

NOW FOR A BLAZE OF PUBLICITY!!!

THE DAILY SUN

31 December 1879

Blaze of glory!

Heroic inventor Thomas A. Edison glowed with pride as he showed off his new invention.

Thousands of people watched him light up the whole town with 3,000 newly-invented light bulbs. Each one looks like a globe of sunshine. No more will people huddle in the dark afraid of the shadows. Thomas Edison is a shining example to the whole nation! It's such a pity that 14 of the new light bulbs have already been pinched.

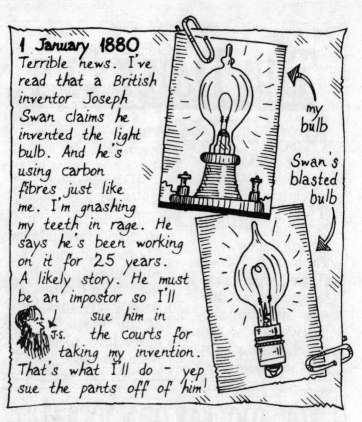

1 January 1880

Terrible news. I've read that a British inventor Joseph Swan claims he invented the light bulb. And he's using carbon fibres just like me. I'm gnashing my teeth in rage. He says he's been working on it for 25 years. A likely story. He must be an impostor so I'll sue him in J.S. the courts for taking my invention. That's what I'll do - yep sue the pants off of him!

my bulb

Swan's blasted bulb

But the British courts found that Swan had indeed been making light bulbs before Edison. Swan was a talented chemist whose inventions included artificial silk. He had finally made a successful carbon filament bulb in February 1879. But he didn't patent the invention because he thought people would copy it anyway.

If you were Thomas Edison what would you do next?

a) Pay Swan $1,000,000 to stop making light bulbs.

b) Try to sell cheaper light bulbs than Swan and drive him out of business.

c) Offer to join forces with Swan.

TEST YOUR TEACHER

Here's your chance to put your teacher under the spotlight. Ask them who invented the light bulb. If they know anything they'll say either Thomas Edison or Joseph Swan – or even both. Shake your head sadly and say:

As so often happens in science, the answer gets more complicated the more you find out. Several inventors made carbon filament lights before Swan and Edison. For example, Scottish inventor James Bowman Lindsay made one in 1835. But he didn't tell many people about it. Apparently, he didn't think there would be money in the new invention. And anyway, scientists have continued to improve on Edison's original design. Yes, it really does take quite a few scientists to invent a light bulb…

A BRIGHTER IDEA

A modern light bulb uses a coiled tungsten metal filament surrounded by argon – a harmless gas found in the air.

FILAMENT

THE ARGON GAS ACTS AS A BUILT IN FIRE EXTINGUISHER

ARGH! I'M 'ARGON'ER

FLUTTER

Modern heat resistant tungsten wires were developed by American William D. Coolidge (1873–1975) (yes, he really did live to 102). The idea of using a gas in the bulb came from another American, Irving Langmuir (1881–1957).

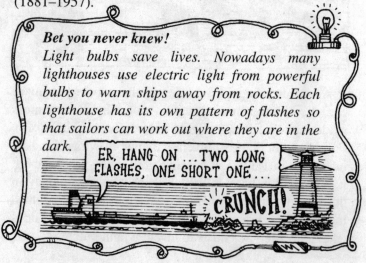

Bet you never knew!
Light bulbs save lives. Nowadays many lighthouses use electric light from powerful bulbs to warn ships away from rocks. Each lighthouse has its own pattern of flashes so that sailors can work out where they are in the dark.

ER, HANG ON ...TWO LONG FLASHES, ONE SHORT ONE...

CRUNCH!

Of course, you'll find bulbs in lots of other places – you might even own a few yourself. Like in your bike lights or your torch.

Take a closer look at any of them and you'll find another amazing light gadget. What is it? A mirror of course, and it's there to reflect the light from the bulb outwards in the direction you want it to go in. And oddly enough, you'll find quite a few mirrors in the next frightening chapter.

FRIGHTENING REFLECTIONS

What's hard, and so shiny you can see your face in it?

No, it's NOT your teacher's bald head.

It's a mirror. When light hits a mirror an amazing thing happens. Light seems to bounce off it to form an image that we call a reflection. Oh, so you knew that already? Well, get this – reflections are unbelievably vital for light science. And they pop up in the most unlikely places.

Why not reflect on this quiz for a moment?

SPOT THE REFLECTION QUIZ

Reflections can help…

1 Road signs glow in the dark. TRUE/FALSE

2 Clouds glow in the sky. TRUE/FALSE

3 A TV set show pictures. TRUE/FALSE

4 A shellfish see. TRUE/FALSE

5 A doctor peer inside your eyeball. TRUE/FALSE

6 A mirage appear. TRUE/FALSE

7 Astronomers detect a black hole in space. TRUE/FALSE

8 The snow blind you. TRUE/FALSE

9 A surgeon peer inside your body without cutting you open. TRUE/FALSE

Answers:

1 TRUE. You can find tiny mirrors in road signs and in road studs. The mirrors reflect car headlights. **2 TRUE.** Clouds reflect sunlight. That's what makes them bright and glowing. Thunderclouds appear dark and gloomy from the ground because they are thicker than ordinary clouds and reflect most of the sunlight upwards. Clouds that glow at night do so because they are high enough in the sky to still catch the sunlight. **3 FALSE.** There are no mirrors inside a TV set. **4 TRUE.** Scallops are a type of shellfish with tiny mirrors in their eyes. Each eye has a shiny layer of crystals that reflect light on to cells inside the eye. A scientist made this discovery whilst looking down a microscope at the shellfish. He saw his own face reflected in the creature's 100 gruesome eyes. **5 TRUE.** A doctor uses an ophthalmoscope (op-thal-mo-scope) to peer inside your eyeball. This instrument shines a light on to a curved mirror that focuses the light beam into your eyeball. The doctor then peers through a hole in the middle of the mirror to inspect your nerves and blood vessels. **6 FALSE.** Mirages are caused by refraction. (Just to remind you, refraction is bended light.) **7 FALSE.** Light can't escape from a black hole (that's why they're black). So you can't spot one with a mirror. **8 TRUE.** Snow reflects light so well that you can be blinded by staring at it for too long in bright sunlight. That's why skiers wear protective goggles. **9 TRUE.** The tube is called an endoscope and it's basically two bundles of optical fibres. One bundle takes light from a light source at one end into the body – just imagine sticking a torch down your throat. The surgeon looks through the other bundle to get a close-up of your innards. And talking about optical fibres…

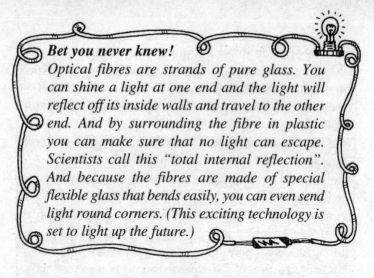

Bet you never knew!

Optical fibres are strands of pure glass. You can shine a light at one end and the light will reflect off its inside walls and travel to the other end. And by surrounding the fibre in plastic you can make sure that no light can escape. Scientists call this "total internal reflection". And because the fibres are made of special flexible glass that bends easily, you can even send light round corners. (This exciting technology is set to light up the future.)

All right, this is what reflections can do. But how do you make reflections to begin with?

Frightening light fact file

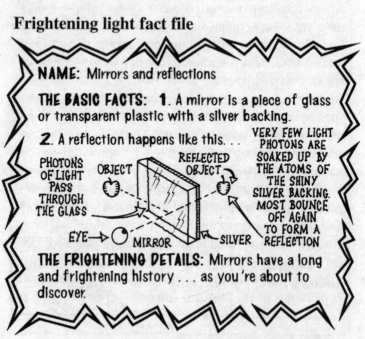

NAME: Mirrors and reflections

THE BASIC FACTS: 1. A mirror is a piece of glass or transparent plastic with a silver backing.

2. A reflection happens like this. . .

PHOTONS OF LIGHT PASS THROUGH THE GLASS

OBJECT

REFLECTED OBJECT

VERY FEW LIGHT PHOTONS ARE SOAKED UP BY THE ATOMS OF THE SHINY SILVER BACKING. MOST BOUNCE OFF AGAIN TO FORM A REFLECTION

EYE → MIRROR — SILVER

THE FRIGHTENING DETAILS: Mirrors have a long and frightening history . . . as you're about to discover.

MURDEROUS MIRRORS

• Early people realized that shiny surfaces were great for seeing yourself in. Very handy for helping you brush your hair properly or spot an embarrassing bogie in your nostril.

• In ancient Egypt all sorts of things were used as mirrors including polished metal, wet slates and bowls of water. But none of them was smooth enough to give a clear, bright image. (In order to see your reflection you need a smooth surface so the photons reflect back together – remember?)

• By the time the Romans came along mirrors were much improved. The Romans used glass to make mirrors with a thin backing of tin. Unfortunately, this invention was to cause a few heated moments. According to legend the Greek scientist Archimedes (287–212 BC) used a bank of mirrors to burn Roman ships that were attacking his home city.

Every mirror reflected sunlight on to a single point on the ship. The wood heated up and burst into flames. This is scientifically possible although there's no proof it happened.

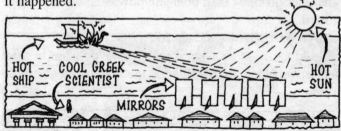

• In the Middle Ages Venice made the finest mirrors in the world. Venetians had learnt to use a mixture of mercury and tin for the backing which was easy to work without heating. This mixture was top secret. A special island was set aside for this work but the mercury was poisonous and many workers died or were driven mad by it. Nevertheless, they were forbidden to pass on the secret on pain of death.

• Somehow by the 1670s the secret had spread to France and then across Europe. In 1840, German chemist, Justus von Liebig (1803–1873) found how to put silver backing on a mirror using heated silver nitrate and other chemicals. And this method is still in use.

• Meanwhile the Chinese had been making excellent mirrors from polished metal for over 2,000 years. Some of these mirrors were called "magic mirrors". Can you solve the riddle of their amazing powers?

COULD YOU BE A SCIENTIST?

You shine a light on a magic mirror. The polished bronze surface reflects back the light on the screen together with a pattern.

But there is no pattern on the surface of the mirror itself. So what causes this strange effect? Only the makers knew the secret. Western and Chinese scientists had been baffled for years. Some Chinese thinkers believed that there was an invisible pattern etched on the front of the mirror that showed up in the reflection.

How would you explain the mirrors?

a) The Chinese thinkers were right. There was a faint pattern on the mirror's surface.

b) The mirrors gave out X-rays that revealed a hidden pattern under the surface.

c) There was a hidden pattern on the back of the mirror that was somehow being reflected from the front.

Answer:

c) The first westerners to find the answer were two British physicists, W.E. Ayrton and J. Perry. In the 1890s they were allowed to visit workshops where the mirrors were made.

1 A PATTERN IS ENGRAVED ON THE BACK OF THE MIRROR

2 THE FRONT SURFACE IS A LAYER OF METAL THAT HAS BEEN SCRAPED UNTIL IT'S VERY THIN

3 LIGHT REFLECTS OFF THE PARTS OF THE SURFACE COVERING THE PATTERN AT A SLIGHTLY DIFFERENT ANGLE TO THE REST OF THE MIRROR

4 THIS CAUSES THE PATTERN TO APPEAR AS DARK LINES ON THE SCREEN

SO WHAT'RE YOU SMILING AT?

The pattern appears as dark lines on the screen.

Bet you never knew!
In the Middle Ages people believed they could see the future by staring at a shiny surface such as a mirror. This practice was known as scrying (sk-ry-ing) – it's the origin of the traditional fortune teller's crystal ball. Other shiny surfaces used were bowls of water or blood.

YOU WILL CROSS THE SEA IN A LARGE BLOOD VESSEL.

And talking about the bad old days…

TEACHER'S TEA-BREAK TEASER

When your grandparents were young, cruel parents and teachers sometimes forced children to shine their shoes until they could see their faces in them. Here's your chance to get a belated revenge. Knock politely on the staffroom door. When it grinds open smile sweetly and enquire…

Note: there's no point in showing your teacher a pair of smelly trainers. Ideally you should be holding a nice pair of shiny shoes for their inspection.

SHINY SHOES   SMELLY TRAINERS

Answer:
Like any non-shiny object, leather is naturally bumpy and reflects light in all directions. That's why you can't see a clear reflection in it. The polish fills in the tiny dips in the leather to make a nice smooth surface that reflects light well and looks jolly smart.

Dare you discover … what a mirror does to light?

You will need:
A mirror
Two eyebrows and yourself

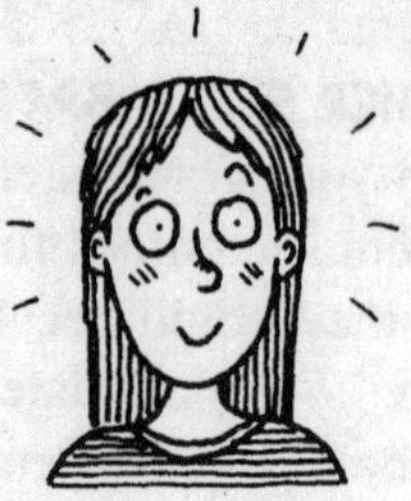

What you do:
1 Stand in front of the mirror.
2 Raise your left eyebrow. (If you can't do this just point to your left eyebrow instead.)

What does your reflection do?
a) It raises its left eyebrow.
b) The reflection raises its right eyebrow.
c) The reflection raises its right eyebrow but there's a delay of about half a second.

Answer:
Here's a great teacher teaser: all you have to do is wave a mirror in front of their ugly mug and challenge them to explain why their face appears the wrong way round. In fact the mirror simply reflects the light from a face. So the reflection of your right eyebrow appears on the right side of your reflected image. Normally when you face someone, you see their right eyebrow on the left of their face as you look at it – and that's why a reflected face appears "the wrong way round". If you really want to torture your teacher you can next ask them to explain quantum electrodynamics (QED for short). This is the mathematical theory that explains how atoms swap photons to create a reflection.

One of the first scientists to investigate reflection was born long ago in what is now Iraq. Europeans call him Alhazen but his proper name was Abu al-Hassan ibn al-Haytham. Here's his story…

Hall of fame: Ibn al-Haytham (965–1040)
Nationality: Arab

Although he was a great scientist al-Haytham was unlucky enough to serve a mad ruler – Egyptian Caliph al-Hakim (985–1021).

According to an old story, one day the scientist boasted to the Caliph that he could build a dam across the River Nile. Big mistake. The Caliph sent al-Haytham to southern Egypt but there he realized there was no suitable site for the dam. There were too many waterfalls. When al-Haytham returned to admit failure the Caliph was furious. He made the scientist stand on a bench and he had the bench hacked to pieces. The Caliph made it horribly clear that al-Haytham was lucky not to be hacked to pieces himself.

IT SHOULD HAVE BEEN YOU FOR THE CHOP!

The Caliph gave al-Haytham an obscure government job. But the Caliph was not a man to cross and the scientist decided on a plan to save his life. He pretended to go mad. Al-Haytham was locked up and the Caliph forgot to have him killed. Ironically, a few years later the Caliph went mad himself and was murdered by an unknown hand. Afterwards al-Haytham told everyone that he had just been pretending.

THE BORING TRUTH?

Of course, some boring historians say this is a story that people told after the scientist's death. Al-Haytham never mentioned it in any of his writings. But then why should he? He'd probably have wanted to forget the incident. And why should he risk raking up the past? What do you think?

The scientist got a job teaching at the Azhar mosque and copying ancient Greek manuscripts. And there he became interested in light. So he wrote a book called *The Treasury of Optics* in which he described his brilliant discoveries. (Unfortunately, he didn't describe his experiments in any detail.)

The Treasury of Optics
by Ibn al-Haytham

I'm not one to boast but I'm forced to admit that I am a brilliant scientist. I have found secrets about light that no one has ever discovered before. And what's more, I have proved all this by mathematical calculations and through experiments using mirrors that I made with my very own hands.

1. Light is given out by glowing objects. Some of the ancient Greek writers believed that light came from the eye and it was this that made the object glow. But I, Ibn al-Haytham have proved them all wrong!

2. Light travels in a straight line. Now as I said, I'm not one to blow my own trumpet - but this was one of my most ingenious and clever experiments. I made a hole in my wall so that the shaft of light entered the room. Then I checked the shaft of light and found it was perfectly straight. Brilliant!

3. Light always reflects at a predictable angle. By the most careful and painstaking measurements worthy only of the highest genius I have proved that if light shines from the left of a mirror it will bounce off to the right or vice-versa. And always at the same mathematically predictable angle.

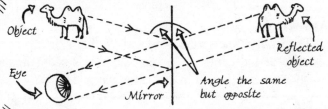

Object

Reflected object

Eye

Mirror

Angle the same but opposite

Although I'm really a very humble, modest person I am sure the name of Ibn al-Haytham will live for ever in history and all the world will want to read of my discoveries!

But people elsewhere in the world weren't interested in light and it took 200 years for al-Haytham's book to even appear in the West. Could you be a scientist like al-Haytham and discover the secrets of reflections? Here's your chance…

Dare you discover … how mirrors can change your appearance?

You will need:
A shiny tablespoon

What you do:
1 Hold the spoon like a hand mirror.
2 Look in the back of the spoon and then the front.

What do you notice?
a) My face appears upside-down in the back of the spoon and the right way up in the front.
b) My face appears fatter in the back of the spoon and upside-down with a long neck in the front of the spoon.
c) My face appears normal in the back of the spoon. In the front of the spoon I'm the right way up but I have a huge hooter.

Answer:
b) The front of the spoon is concave – that is it curves inwards at the centre. (To remember this word just imagine a cave shaped in the same way.)

CONCAVE SPOON
CONCAVE CAVE

Because of this shape, light reflecting from your face reflects downwards from the top of the spoon and upwards from the bottom.

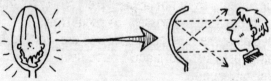

You see the bottom of your face at the top of the spoon and the top at the bottom. And your face appears upside-down. Turn the spoon around and you're faced with a bulging or as scientists say a convex shape.

BULGING CENTRE
BULGING TUMMY

CONVEX MIRROR   CONVEX SCIENTIST

The convex shape reflects the light from your face and spreads it slightly outwards. This makes your face appear rounder and fatter (though ths time you're the right way up!).

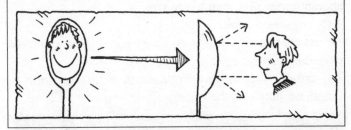

HORRIBLE HEALTH WARNING!

Your parents may not appreciate you performing this interesting experiment at meal times. Especially when the posh relatives are waiting for their brussels sprouts and you're using the best silver tablespoon.

Dare you discover ... how to make a ghost appear?

(This experiment is so good you'll want to do it again and again. All in the interests of Science, of course.)

You will need:

Sticky tape

Scissors

A small but bright torch

A mirror – about 24 cm x 36 cm is ideal.

A piece of black paper (larger than your mirror).

A pencil

A large black water-based felt-tip marker.

A room with light-coloured walls.

What you do:

1 Draw the outline of your ghost on the black paper. This should be smaller than the mirror.

2 Cut out the outline.

3 Stick the remaining paper with the ghost shape removed over the mirror.

4 Use the felt tip to draw in the features of your ghost in the ghost shape on the mirror.

5 Darken the room. Better still wait until nightfall – after all, that's when ghosts appear.

6 Prop the mirror securely on an arm chair. The [mirror] should be facing the wall about two metres away. Shin[e] your torch at the mirror. Your ghost appears on the wall.

7 Move the torch so the ghost appears to float in the air.

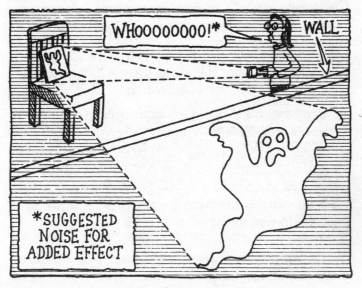

What is the scientific explanation for the ghost?

a) The torch light reflects off the black paper and the felt tip lines.

b) The light reflects off the mirror but not the paper or the lines.

c) The light reflects off everything.

HORRIBLE HEALTH WARNING!

1 Don't try this experiment until you've checked with your parents it's OK to draw on the mirror. Defacing your granny's priceless antique mirror could prove fatal.

2 Be careful when handling the mirror. Mirrors are glass (surprise, surprise) and they can break and injure people. And give you seven years bad luck, so it's said.

DRAT! I HAVEN'T BROKEN A MIRROR FOR SIX YEARS, ELEVEN MONTHS AND THIRTY DAYS

SMASH!

CRIKEY, THAT'S BAD LUCK, THEN!

3 Make sure the felt-tip pen is water based. It should be possible to wipe the ink off with water.

Whilst we're talking about frightening things, I should warn you about the next chapter. Beware – lurking among the weird facts in the chapter is a sinister-looking spider.

Will it frighten the socks off you? Read on and find out…

ARGH!

FRIGHTENING LIGHT-BENDERS

What have all these things got in common?

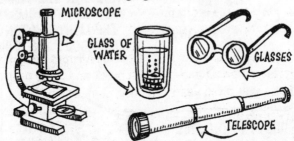

Yes, I know they all contain glass but that *isn't* the only CORRECT answer. Give up? Well, the other answer is that they all bend or refract light. But how do they do it?

Well, bend your eyes to this...

Frightening light fact file

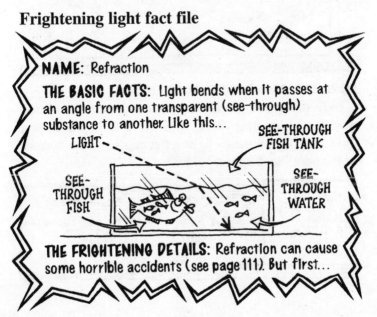

NAME: Refraction

THE BASIC FACTS: Light bends when it passes at an angle from one transparent (see-through) substance to another. Like this...

THE FRIGHTENING DETAILS: Refraction can cause some horrible accidents (see page 111). But first...

Here's a slow-motion replay of refraction as light hits that fish tank.

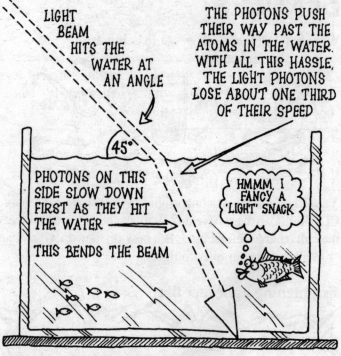

LIGHT BEAM HITS THE WATER AT AN ANGLE

THE PHOTONS PUSH THEIR WAY PAST THE ATOMS IN THE WATER. WITH ALL THIS HASSLE, THE LIGHT PHOTONS LOSE ABOUT ONE THIRD OF THEIR SPEED

45°

PHOTONS ON THIS SIDE SLOW DOWN FIRST AS THEY HIT THE WATER →

THIS BENDS THE BEAM

HMMM, I FANCY A 'LIGHT' SNACK

HORRIBLE REFRACTION ACCIDENTS

1 Ever stared straight down into a swimming pool and wondered how deep it is? Well, it's deeper than you think. Refraction bends light reflecting from the bottom of the pool. So it appears closer.

I'M JUST GOING FOR A PADDLE, MUM...

2 Told you…

3 You can see this effect if you stare down at your legs in the water. They appear stumpy and short. It's true – honest, I'm not pulling your leg.

4 In South America, and parts of the Pacific and Africa people fish with spears but thanks to refraction the fish often get away. And accidents do happen…

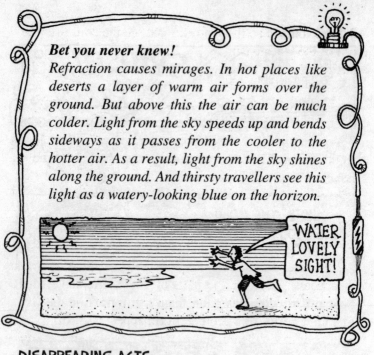

WATER LOVELY SIGHT!

DISAPPEARING ACTS

But refraction can do even weirder things. Like making objects disappear. Oh, so you don't believe me, well, try this...

Dare you discover ... how to make a coin disappear?

You will need:
A £1 coin
A wash basin
A ruler

OK, AS LONG AS IT DOESN'T DISAPPEAR DOWN THE SWEETSHOP

What you do:
1 Fill the basin with water to a depth of 4 cm.
2 Place the coin in the water.

3 Crouch down so that you can just see the coin over the rim of the wash basin.

4 Lift the plug slightly so the water level in the sink falls slowly.

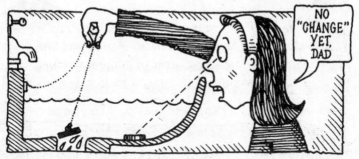

As the water drains down the plug hole the coin gradually disappears. *Why?*

a) Grrrr! My coin has gone down the drain!

b) The water refracted the light reflecting back from the coin so it made the coin look further away than it really was.

c) The light from the coin was refracted so the coin appeared closer.

Answer:
c) The water bent the light towards you so the coin appeared closer. As the water drained away the light refracted less. The coin appeared to move away until it disappeared behind the rim. But actually the coin didn't move.

If refraction can make coins vanish then maybe it can make a larger object disappear. Perhaps even a human being? Here's a story in which this happens – but is it true? What do you think?

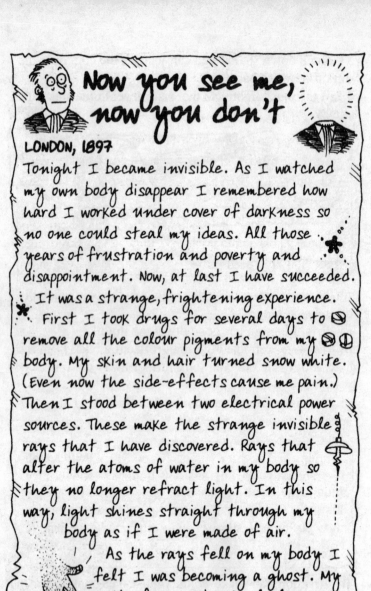

Now you see me, now you don't

LONDON, 1897

Tonight I became invisible. As I watched my own body disappear I remembered how hard I worked under cover of darkness so no one could steal my ideas. All those years of frustration and poverty and disappointment. Now, at last I have succeeded.

It was a strange, frightening experience. First I took drugs for several days to remove all the colour pigments from my body. My skin and hair turned snow white. (Even now the side-effects cause me pain.) Then I stood between two electrical power sources. These make the strange invisible rays that I have discovered. Rays that alter the atoms of water in my body so they no longer refract light. In this way, light shines straight through my body as if I were made of air.

As the rays fell on my body I felt I was becoming a ghost. My white face and hair slowly grew dimmer until I could see nothing

114

in the mirror. The skin of my arms and legs looked like glass – I could see the fat and nerves beneath.

And gradually everything faded away until I could stand before the mirror and see nothing but an empty room. . .

Answer:
Great story, isn't it? It's based on *The Invisible Man* by H.G. Wells (1866–1946). But it's only a story because: 1 The rays described don't exist. 2 If the scientist had no pigments then he wouldn't have pigments in his retina to help him see. 3 The lens and cornea of the eye refract light and focus it on to the retina. (Remember that bit from page 45?) But if the scientist's invisible body didn't refract light then these bits of his eye wouldn't refract it either. So he couldn't see the room.

BRILLIANT LENSES

Assuming you're not invisible, lenses are a brilliant way to refract light. They come in two main varieties, convex and concave. (Remember these words?)

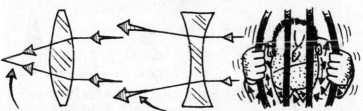

CONVEX LENS LIGHT BENDS INWARDS   CONCAVE LENS LIGHT BENDS OUTWARDS   CONVICT LEN BENDS BARS

OK, let's take a peek through these lenses. And here's a particularly revolting hairy spider to study…

1 Through a convex lens the spider appears bigger. Let's take a look at the spider's head.

2 Light reflects off the spider's ugly little mug.

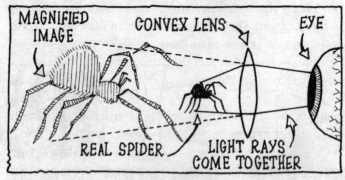

The convex lens bends this light towards a single point.

3 If you put your eye at this point you'll see a close-up view of the spider's head with eight huge beady eyes staring back at you. YIKES!

Let's use a concave lens to take another look at the spider. Yes, it's all in the interests of Science.

1 This lens spreads the light wider.

2 And when you look through the lens the spider appears much smaller. Phew! Not so bad – eh?

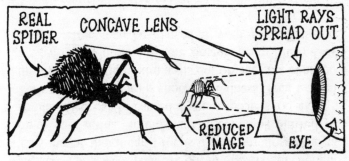

So concave lenses make things look smaller and convex lenses make them look bigger. And not surprisingly you find convex lenses in cameras, binoculars, telescopes, microscopes and loads of scientific instruments which make things appear larger.

Of course, if you're wearing glasses to read this page you'll know all about lenses. You've got two of them perched on the end of your nose. But why wear them?

FRIGHTENING EXPRESSIONS

An ophthalmologist says…

YOU MAY HAVE HYPEROPIA, MYOPIA OR ASTIGMATISM

Are any of these fatal?

Answer:

No, they're eye problems caused by faulty focusing.

1 Hyperopia (hi-per-rop-pia) means that you're long-sighted. The lens of your eye doesn't bend light enough. This means that it can't focus light from close objects on to your retina. So close up objects look blurred. A similar effect can be caused if your eyeball is too short.

2 Myopia (mi-ope-ia) is short-sightedness. That's when the light reflecting from a distant object gets bent too far by your lens and distant objects seem blurred. A similar effect can be caused if your eyeball is too long.

3 Astigmatism (as-stig-ma-tism) is when the cornea is slightly out of shape. This results in part of the image appearing blurred.

If you've got any of these you'll need to wear glasses or contact lenses to correct the problem. Cheer up you'll look dead brainy and they're scientifically fascinating…

SPECTACULAR SPECTACLES

1 The first glasses to be invented had convex lenses. They were probably invented in Italy in the thirteenth century and worn by long-sighted people.

2 As you've just discovered, the long-sighted eye has a lens that doesn't bend the light inwards enough to focus an image on the retina.

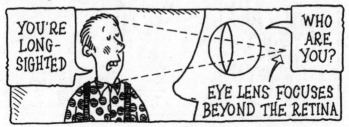

A convex lens bends the light further inwards to focus an image.

3 Concave lenses were first made in around 1451. German churchman Nicholas of Cusa (1401–1464) worked out that this shape could help short-sighted people. What a far-sighted man!

4 A short-sighted eye lens pushes the light inwards too much. So the light focuses before it gets to the retina.

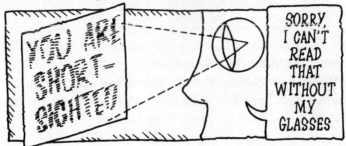

The concave lens spreads the light so it focuses on the retina.

5 Contact lenses do the same job as glasses. Nowadays they're slices of soft watery plastic that fit over the eyeball. But the first lenses invented by German Adolf Fick (1829–1901) in 1888 were made of glass. The glass rubbed against the eyeballs and made them sore. What a sight for sore eyes!

6 And Adolf even managed to make lenses of exactly the right shape to fit over the eyeball and bend light on to the retina. The answer was to shape the lenses in moulds made by using the eyeballs of dead people.

7 DON'T WORRY! Your local optician DOESN'T have a drawer full of eyeballs. Nowadays, they measure the curve of your eyeballs using a keratometer (ker-rato-meter). This instrument directs a beam of light into your eyeball (which reflects it) and records the position of the reflected light. This data is used to calculate its exact curve.

8 Not surprisingly, it was a pair of spectacle makers who found a new use for their lenses. In 1608 Dutch spectacle maker, Hans Lippershey (1570–1618) invented the telescope and soon afterwards his assistant Zacharius Jannsen (1580–1638) invented the microscope. Or did they?

Bet you never knew!
Hans Lippershey got the idea for the telescope after watching two children playing with his lenses. The children placed two convex lenses at a distance and they found they could see their local church steeple in amazing detail. Apparently neither Hans nor anyone else had tried this experiment. The Dutch government gave Hans 900 florins for his invention but the poor children didn't get a peek at the money (not even through a telescope).

DRAT, IT'S THOSE KIDS. I'D BETTER HIDE THE MONEY.

Anyway, talking about telescopes…

FRIGHTENING EXPRESSIONS…

ARGH! IT'S CHROMATIC ABERRATION!

Sounds frightening. Could this mean the end of the world? No. Chromatic aberration means he's got a problem with his telescope. It's caused by different-size light waves being refracted by different amounts.

A traditional telescope has two or more convex lenses.

The lenses focus light from a distant object on to your eyeball.

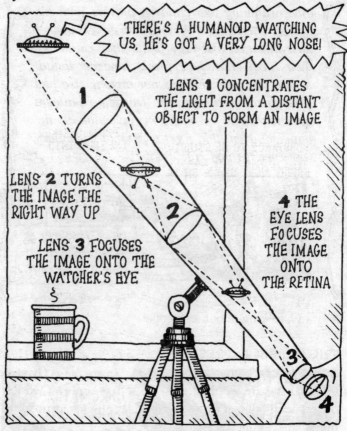

But here's the problem. Because different coloured lights refract at different angles, they don't all focus in exactly the same spot. So images would have a coloured "halo"around the edge – and that's chromatic aberration.

Luckily for astronomers, Isaac Newton solved this problem in 1668. He designed a telescope that used a concave mirror to focus the light instead of a lens.

Because mirrors reflect all wavelengths in the same way, there was no "halo" around the image. And Newton's design is still in use today.

Bet you never knew!
Telescopes aren't just for watching the stars or seeing things in the distance. You'll also find a telescope in a scientific instrument called a spectroscope.

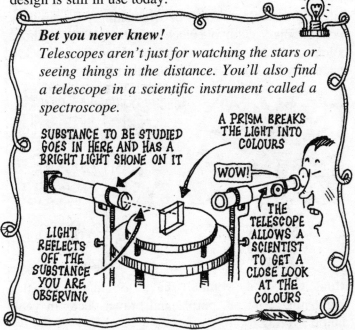

A PRISM BREAKS THE LIGHT INTO COLOURS

SUBSTANCE TO BE STUDIED GOES IN HERE AND HAS A BRIGHT LIGHT SHONE ON IT

WOW!

LIGHT REFLECTS OFF THE SUBSTANCE YOU ARE OBSERVING

THE TELESCOPE ALLOWS A SCIENTIST TO GET A CLOSE LOOK AT THE COLOURS

Talking of colours you'd better read the next chapter. It's full of crucial colourful facts. Yep, colour is CRUCIAL – I mean, where would drivers be if they couldn't tell the difference between a green and a red light? In hospital that's where!

Well, you've got the green light to turn over the page.

READY STEADY TURN!

CRUCIAL COLOURS

Life without colour would be frighteningly boring. Just like an endless awful, old black and white movie. Without colour you'd never get to enjoy the glory of a peacock's tail, a glowing sunset or a garden full of flowers.

Mind you, you wouldn't have to shudder at the frightening crimson, purple and brown decor in your auntie's living room.

A NOTE TO THE READER

We apologize for the loss of colour. Readers will have to imagine the wonderful glowing, vibrant colours described in these pages. And if you do get bored you can always colour them in. **PS** If it's not your book go and buy your own before you pick up your crayons. Anyway, here's how light makes colour appear.

Frightening light fact file

NAME: Colours

THE BASIC FACTS: 1. White light is a muddled-up mix of all the colours of the rainbow and each colour is made of a light wave with a different frequency (energy level). Remember all that?

2. When light hits an object some of the colours are soaked up and others are reflected. And it's the reflected colours that we see. Got all that?

THE FRIGHTENING DETAILS: When something is black all the colours in light are soaked up so nothing reflects back. This explains the colour of this big black revolting slug.

YEAH, CHEERS!

Read on for more colourful facts.

THE COLOURFUL FACTS

A green leaf or caterpillar soaks up all the colours in light except green. Green reflects off the leaf (or caterpillar) and that's what you see.

GREEN PLANT

GARDENER'S GREEN FINGERS

GREEN CATERPILLAR

A ripe tomato soaks up all kinds of light except red.

White objects reflect every kind of light. (Don't forget white light is all the colours mixed up.)

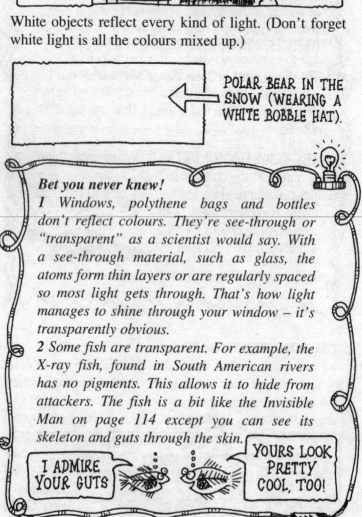

POLAR BEAR IN THE SNOW (WEARING A WHITE BOBBLE HAT).

Bet you never knew!

1 Windows, polythene bags and bottles don't reflect colours. They're see-through or "transparent" as a scientist would say. With a see-through material, such as glass, the atoms form thin layers or are regularly spaced so most light gets through. That's how light manages to shine through your window – it's transparently obvious.

2 Some fish are transparent. For example, the X-ray fish, found in South American rivers has no pigments. This allows it to hide from attackers. The fish is a bit like the Invisible Man on page 114 except you can see its skeleton and guts through the skin.

I ADMIRE YOUR GUTS

YOURS LOOK PRETTY COOL, TOO!

Dare you discover … where colour comes from?

You will need:

A nice juicy red tomato
A piece of white A4 paper
A small but bright torch

What you do:

1 Darken the room or better still wait for nightfall.
2 Place the tomato on one end of the paper.
3 Hold the torch over the paper level with the tomato. Shine the light on the tomato.

4 Look at the area of shadow under the torch beam. It should be glowing pink. *Why?*

a) The tomato is reflecting red light on to the paper.

b) It's a trick of my eyes caused by the torch light.

c) The shadow of the tomato is soaking up all the colours in light except red.

Answer:
a) White paper reflects all the colours of light that fall on it. The pink glow is due to the red light reflecting off the tomato and on to the paper. All the other colours in the light get soaked up by the tomato. The experiment proves that colours are indeed caused by the reflection of light.

127

Most objects, though, reflect a mix of different coloured light. Take bananas, for example…

DON'T TAKE ANY OF MINE!

TEACHER'S TEA-BREAK TEASER

You will need a banana and a lot of courage. Rap smartly on the staffroom door. When it squeaks open put on your most innocent expression and enquire…

WHAT COLOUR IS THIS BANANA?

HUH?

STA

Answer:
Well, it might appear yellow but it actually reflects red and green light and soaks up blue light. Your eyes see this mix of red and green as yellow. (You can find out how on pages 136-137.)

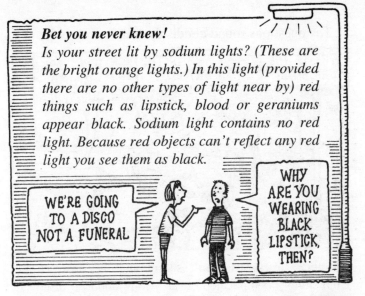

Bet you never knew!

Is your street lit by sodium lights? (These are the bright orange lights.) In this light (provided there are no other types of light near by) red things such as lipstick, blood or geraniums appear black. Sodium light contains no red light. Because red objects can't reflect any red light you see them as black.

WE'RE GOING TO A DISCO NOT A FUNERAL

WHY ARE YOU WEARING BLACK LIPSTICK, THEN?

Talking about reflecting colours, did you know two scientists spent their holidays reflecting on this very topic? That's sad.

Hall of fame: Chandrasekhara Vankata Raman
(1888–1970) Nationality: Indian
John Strutt, Lord Rayleigh (1824–1919)
Nationality: British

You couldn't find two more different characters than C.V. Raman and John Strutt.

Raman was a brilliant scientist but he had to work for the Indian civil service as a young man because of a shortage of scientific jobs in India. (In 1917 he became Professor of Physics at Calcutta University.) Strutt was a rich lord with a private laboratory in his mansion and a top university job in England. They worked separately to solve two tricky light questions but by an odd coincidence Raman later became friendly with Strutt's son.

The questions sound childishly simple…

But these questions aren't stupid and the answers are frighteningly complicated … as you're about to discover. In 1871 John Strutt went on holiday to Egypt. Cruising through the Mediterranean, he admired the lovely blue sky and sea.

Being a scientist, though, he did more than enjoy what he saw. He used his scientific know-how to explain it. His letter home might have read like this…

To Lord & Lady Rayleigh,
Tering Place, Essex, England.

Dear Mum and Dad,
Having a great holiday! I've read lots
of science books and there's plenty
of interesting sights to fascinate a
budding scientist like me. Like the
blue sky and sea, for example. I
mean, what makes them so blue? I
suspect atoms in the air reflect
light. I think blue light is
scattered much better than other
lights (I'm not sure why) so we see
more of it. I reckon the sea is blue
because it reflects the sky.
    Oh, I forgot to say, the cruise is OK.
Yours scientifically,
John

NOTES TO THE READER...

1 John was right. Blue light photons have more energy
and this makes them more likely to bounce off the atoms
downwards and into our eyes. So we get to see more blue
light photons when we look at the sky. And that makes
the sky appear blue. Honest, it's a true-blue fact!.

2 But sunsets aren't blue – are they? Well, this actually
proves John Strutt was right. When the sun is low we
see its light shining at an angle through all the grotty old
dust in the air. The dust reflects away most of the blue

photons before the light gets to us. But who cares? We get to enjoy the reddish-orange colours that were in the sunlight and didn't get reflected upwards so much.

OK, now back to the story…

In 1921, Raman was sailing to a Science conference in Britain. Feeling rather bored he decided to test John Strutt's findings about the sea. By this time the older scientist was dead so Raman couldn't drop him a postcard. But he might have written to his pal John Strutt's scientist son, Robert Strutt, the next Lord Rayleigh (1875–1947).

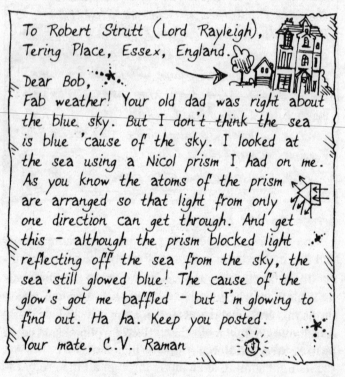

To Robert Strutt (Lord Rayleigh), Tering Place, Essex, England.

Dear Bob,
Fab weather! Your old dad was right about the blue sky. But I don't think the sea is blue 'cause of the sky. I looked at the sea using a Nicol prism I had on me. As you know the atoms of the prism are arranged so that light from only one direction can get through. And get this – although the prism blocked light reflecting off the sea from the sky, the sea still glowed blue! The cause of the glow's got me baffled – but I'm glowing to find out. Ha ha. Keep you posted.
Your mate, C.V. Raman

So why *was* the sea blue?

132

Back at his lab in 1922 Raman did a series of experiments that involved shining light through water and found the answer...

Dear Bob,
I've cracked it. I was looking into why the sea is blue – remember? Well, here's what I've found out:
1. Part of the light from the sky is reflected by the surface of the sea. OK – your dad got that bit right. That's why the sea is grey when the sky is dark and cloudy. But lots of photons get into the sea itself...
2. The seawater soaks up most of these photons and only reflects back blue light photons. This is the blue glow I saw.
I'm sure your old dad would have been chuffed.
Your Pal,
C.V. Raman

blue sky

blue photons   *light photons*

blue glow

For Raman, it must have seemed that the sky (and the sea) was the limit. He went on to find how bonds between atoms in a chemical can affect an atom's wobble and add or remove energy from the reflecting photons. And in 1930 he won the Nobel Prize for this work.

MYSTERIOUS COLOUR MIXING

On their own, colours are fairly straightforward. But try mixing them together and the facts get murky.

Bet you never knew!

Colour photos are made by mixing different light colours.

1 The first colour picture was taken by Scottish physicist James Clerk Maxwell (1831–1879). In 1863 he took three snaps of one of his wife's ribbons. One through a red filter, one blue and one green. Each filter blocked all the colours in light except its particular colour. So the green filter, for example, showed up the green parts of the pattern. He combined the images to make a colour picture.

FASCINATING, CAN I HAVE IT BACK NOW?

2 Nowadays, though, colour films consist of three layers of chemicals. The top layer makes a blue colour from blue light, the second makes green in the same way and the third makes a red colour. Between them the chemicals build up an image. Our brains do the rest of the colour mixing – as you'll discover on pages 136–137.

MUDDY MIXED-UP PAINTS

But just imagine that you tried to make a painting in the same way as a photo. You carefully mixed thin layers of blue, green and red. And produced a muddy black smear.

I CALL THIS, "FLY'S VIEW OF A COWPAT"

Want to know why? Why not ask your art teacher…

TEST YOUR ART TEACHER

If you mix green and red and blue light together you'll get a pale whitish sort of a colour. But if you mix together green and red and blue paints you get black – why?

Answer:
White light is made up of all colours. So the more colours of light you mix the closer you get to white light. But paints and other coloured objects (like tomatoes and bananas) work by soaking up some light colours and reflecting others. So the more paints you add to your mix the closer you get to something that soaks up every colour in light. In other words – black.

YOU'VE ADDED MORE PAINT

YES. NOW IT'S CALLED, "BLACK CAT IN A POWERCUT"

CRUCIAL COLOUR VISION

Whatever colours you manage to mix you'll need a pair of eyes to appreciate them. Humans, birds and apes are lucky in this respect. We view the world in glorious living Technicolor. Unlike for example, a squid, which can only see black and white or your pet cat who sees green and blue and violet but not red. (Scientists aren't quite sure why this is – but when Tiddles finishes off a mouse she sees the blood and gory bits as green.)

ALL OF A SUDDEN... I DON'T FEEL HUNGRY

HOW YOU SEE IN COLOUR

1 Unlike Tiddles you've actually got three types of cone cells in your retina – one each for green, blue and red light. All the colours you see are made from mixing at least two of these colours. (For more info on mixing light see page 128.)

2 Your incredible eyes are able to make out up to ten million different colours. It's amazing to think they can do this from just three basic colours. Here's your chance to test this remarkable ability…

Dare you discover … how you see colours?

You will need:
A piece of black paper
A small piece of yellow paper about 3 cm square.
Your head complete with eyeballs.

What you do:

1 Place the yellow paper on the black paper and stare at it for 30 seconds without moving your head or blinking.

2 You should see a square of blue appearing round the edge of the yellow square.

What do you notice?

a) The cells that fire blue signals take time to work – but now they've detected blue colouring in the black paper.

b) The yellow paper has excited your blue cells so much they've gone into overdrive. And now you're seeing too much blue.

c) The green and red cells that give you yellow are getting tired but the blue cells are still firing.

EYEBALL TO EYEBALL

WARNING: DISGUSTING FACTS COMING UP. (Hopefully your breakfast won't be coming up after you read them.)

Isaac Newton reckoned we see colours by changing the shape of our eyeballs. Isaac thought this helped the eye to refract white light into coloured light that then fell on the retina.

To test this idea Isaac stuck what might have been a toothpick under his eyeball. A toothpick is a stick for getting bits of food out from between your teeth. Isaac's toothpick was probably encrusted with millions of germs and the stale remains of his supper. YUCK!

Using the toothpick Isaac squeezed his own eyeball to change its shape. He saw a few lights, but not enough to prove his theory.

The germs on the toothpick infected his eyeball. It became so painful that he had to go to bed for two weeks. This proves that even a scientific genius can do very stupid things.

HORRIBLE HEALTH WARNING!

So don't try an experiment like this at home. It has no scientific value. And you don't want an eye infection . . . or your eyeball slopping out of its socket, now do you?

MORE COLOURFUL SCIENTISTS...

After Newton, other famous scientists probed colour vision. The story continues with British chemist John Dalton (1766–1844). John Dalton was one of the first people to suggest that there were such things as atoms. But come to think of it, he wasn't too colourful himself.

A fellow scientist said:

HIS STYLE OF WRITING AND CONVERSATION ARE DRY

Nowadays we might call him "boring". Boring John loved to study flowers. Unfortunately, he found that he couldn't see red colours properly...

IT'S BLUE

IT'S RED

NO NEED TO GET ALL BLUE IN THE FACE ABOUT IT

John suffered from colour deficiency – a condition that affects about one in 25 people and he enjoyed giving boring lectures on the subject. According to John colour deficiency was caused by a build up of blue juice in the eyeball. The blue colour soaks up red light.

He made arrangements for his eyeballs to be removed after his death to check for blue juice.

Meanwhile our old pal Thomas Young had been treating patients with colour deficiency. As a result of this work he believed the retina had separate regions that detected red, blue and violet. And Dalton had a problem with his red region.

Unfortunately Young died before Dalton's eyeballs were removed so he never knew the result. In fact, the jelly in Dalton's eyeballs proved to be nice and clear. Dalton would have been dead disappointed if he wasn't already dead.

THE MYSTERY SOLVED...

The mystery was solved by another famous scientist, James Clerk Maxwell. He spun a disc divided into green and red and blue sections. The colours appeared to merge into white. People who couldn't see the colour red saw white in a spinning disc that had only blue and green sections. This proved...

1 That the cone cells in our eyes can see green, blue and red light.

2 That they make all the other colours from these three. (The white colour was a mix of all the other colours.)

3 In colour deficient people one type of cone cell is missing or not working properly.

Bet you never knew!

As long as your vision's working OK you're bound to enjoy a multi-coloured laser show. By using different chemicals in lasers scientists can change the colour of this light. For example, atoms of ruby produce red light. But you can't enjoy the pretty colours by gazing directly into a laser beam. It's so bright it would probably blind you or heat up your eyeball until it boils.

Dare you take a closer look at lasers? Why not turn to the next frightening chapter?

ER, OK THEN...

BLISTERING LASERS

As you're about to find out, lasers are a huge part of modern life and they're set to brighten up our future too. Like all great inventions, lasers began with a flash of inspiration.

A LASER FLASH OF INSPIRATION

In 1951 US scientist Charles H. Townes was at a scientific conference in Washington.

That night Townes couldn't sleep. His mind was working overtime on the problem. So very early the next morning before it got light he went for a walk and ended up on a park bench. He was looking for inspiration.

Suddenly he found it. Townes scribbled his ideas on the back of an old envelope. If you could control the speed the atoms wobble and stop the light escaping you could create a powerful beam of light. Since radio waves are made by photons you could do the same things with radio waves.

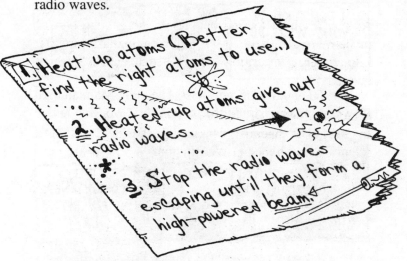

Townes later found out he had been sitting opposite of the house of famous inventor Alexander Graham Bell (1847–1922). And Townes wondered if the dead inventor had provided ghostly assistance.

Later Townes realized that you could use light instead of radio waves. By 1958 working with his brother-in-law, Arthur Schawlow, Townes had worked out how a laser might work. He even coined the name "laser" over lunch. But he had little idea of how useful the laser would become. He later said:

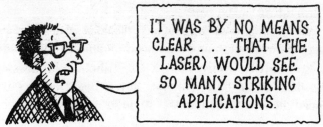

IT WAS BY NO MEANS CLEAR . . . THAT (THE LASER) WOULD SEE SO MANY STRIKING APPLICATIONS.

For scientists at the time, building a laser just seemed a fascinating technical challenge.

In 1960 another US physicist, Theodore Maiman used Townes's plans to build the world's first working laser.

In 1964 Townes won the Nobel Prize for his work together with two Russian scientists, Nikolai Basov and Alexander Prokhorov who developed the laser separately but at the same time.

Interesting postscript:
Actually, unknown to Townes, the idea of a laser and perhaps even the name had been dreamt up by another US scientist, Gordon Gould in 1957. Unfortunately, Gould didn't publish his idea and he didn't take out a patent in time so he missed out on the glory.

LASER DEFENCE SYSTEMS

Lasers have loads of uses. One purpose developed by the US military is a laser defence system to shoot down enemy missiles. Sounds exciting? Well, here's how to defend your school from hostile attack with a laser defence system.

HORRIBLE HEALTH WARNINGS!

1 Laser beams can sizzle human flesh. Do not direct your laser beam anywhere near a teacher or any other poor defenceless creatures.

2 This laser is highly destructive. You can only read this section if you promise to use your laser system to PROTECT your school. And NOT to vaporize the buildings before science class on Monday.

HOW TO MAKE YOUR OWN LASER DEFENCE SYSTEM

TOP SECRET INSTRUCTIONS – KEEP OUT OF REACH OF TEACHERS

Step 1 – assemble your materials.
To build your own laser defence system you will need…
A power supply.
A box lined with mirrors. Leave a partly-silvered mirror in one end for your laser to shine through.
Something to produce light photons (a block of ruby will do).
A bucket of water.
You will also need…
A high-speed jet plane complete with pilot and a

computer controlled high sensitivity heat detecting system. (You may be able to borrow these from your local air force base.)

Step 2 – assemble your laser.

1 Place the ruby in the box and link it up to your power supply.

2 OK, this is the bit that you've been waiting for. Flick the switch and turn on your power supply.

3 The power surge makes the atoms in the ruby wobble violently. They give out photons of red light. These bump into more atoms which wobble and make more photons.

4 A growing crowd of photons charges up and down the inside of the box reflecting off the mirrors. Eventually the light is so bright the photons actually flash *through* the mirror as a blinding beam of light.

5 All this power makes your ruby very hot. If your machine shows signs of over-heating simply chuck the water over it. (Some lasers have built-in water cooling systems.)

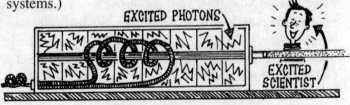

EXCITED PHOTONS

EXCITED SCIENTIST

Step 3 – how to shoot down missiles.

1 Simply get your plane in the air and keep an eye out for incoming missiles. You can use your heat detecting system to track the heat blasting from behind the enemy missile.

2 When you spot a missile aim the laser at its fuel tank. Try to keep the beam steady for a few seconds. The laser's heat will melt the missile's side and set fire to its fuel. The enemy missile will then blow up in mid-air and you'll have saved your school.

EXCELLENT JENKINS. I'LL MAKE SURE YOU GET A GOOD REPORT THIS TERM.

MAKING LIGHT WORK

Of course, your laser can do much more than zap enemy missiles. In fact, lasers can make light work of many jobs...

1 A laser beam makes a snappy-snipper! Lasers are used in factories to cut fabric at 15 m a second.

2 Laser beams read bar codes in shops or libraries. Take a look on the back of this book. Can you see a square with a pattern of lines? The pattern is a unique code for *Frightening Light*. If you bought the book you may have seen the shop assistant passing a scanner across the lines. A laser beam in the scanner flickers as it picks up the lines and the flickering beam is read by a computer that recognizes the code from the pattern of flickers. Here's an idea that's really on the right lines.

3 Lasers can be life-savers. They can cut through human flesh and heat seal the edges of a wound so you don't get bleeding. By firing a laser down an endoscope (that's a tube containing optical fibres, remember) you can perform life-saving operations deep within the body. A laser can even weld back a retina that has come adrift from the inside of the eyeball.

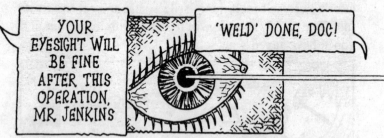

4 A laser beam "reads" a CD by flickering as it reflects off a pattern of pits on its surface. The CD player turns this flickering light signal into electric pulses and then into your fave pop music.

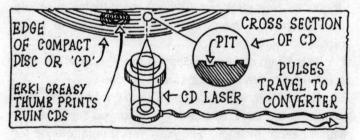

5 Laser beams travel in straight lines so you can use them to build nice straight tunnels. Simply fire a beam from the entrance of the tunnel and get digging along the line of the beam.

6 A laser beam can melt and weld metals. And unlike any other tool a laser beam never gets blunt with use.

148

7 Laser beams liven up pop concerts. Simply fire the laser into the air and wave it around to make dramatic light patterns. And then who cares if the music's rubbish?

8 Lasers can measure tiny earthquakes. Lasers on the San Andreas Fault, California are linked up to monitoring equipment. Any wobble in the light beam caused by a tremor in the ground can be instantly detected.

9 Laser printers work by firing an image of the page you're printing on to a light-sensitive drum. This drum has an electrical force which then picks up toner (the black stuff) and prints on to the paper. And laser printers are fast – maybe that's because they keep in toner – ha ha.

But that's just the start of what lasers can do … they're so useful that scientists have really taken a shine to them, ha, ha.

Bet you never knew!
You can make holograms with lasers. All you have to do is…

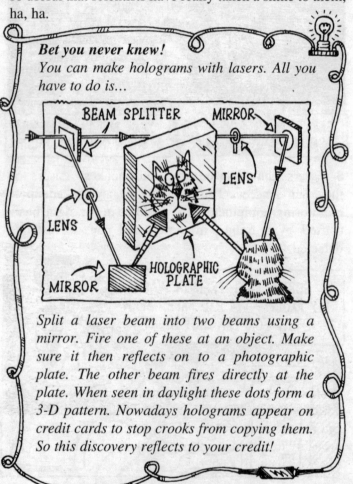

Split a laser beam into two beams using a mirror. Fire one of these at an object. Make sure it then reflects on to a photographic plate. The other beam fires directly at the plate. When seen in daylight these dots form a 3-D pattern. Nowadays holograms appear on credit cards to stop crooks from copying them. So this discovery reflects to your credit!

SPEEDY SIGNALS

Don't forget light is *FAST* with a capital F. And so is laser light.

• In 0.14 seconds you can send a laser signal around the world.

OUCH! I TOLD YOU TO POINT THAT LASER AWAY FROM ME!

I DID BUT IT WENT ROUND THE WORLD AND SHOT YOU IN THE BUM

• In 2.5 seconds you can send a light signal to the moon *and* back again. (In the 1960s US scientists did this. By timing the signal they were able to calculate the exact distance of the moon.)

• A laser could send a light signal to Mars in just three minutes. (The Martians' reply would take another three minutes.)

THIS IS PLANET EARTH. . . IS THERE ANYTHING TO EAT ON YOUR WORLD?

3 MINUTES

YES EARTHLINGS – MARZ BARS, MARZIPAN, AND MARTIAN MALLOWS

But laser signals aren't just for chatting with aliens. You probably use them to natter to your friends. Yes – every time you pick up a phone.

LISTENING LASERS

When you talk into a phone connected to an optical fibre cable the same technology that turns a laser light into sound in a CD works in reverse.

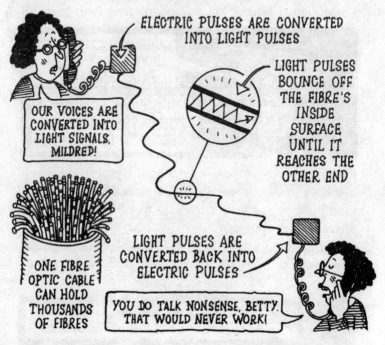

ELECTRIC PULSES ARE CONVERTED INTO LIGHT PULSES

OUR VOICES ARE CONVERTED INTO LIGHT SIGNALS, MILDRED!

LIGHT PULSES BOUNCE OFF THE FIBRE'S INSIDE SURFACE UNTIL IT REACHES THE OTHER END

ONE FIBRE OPTIC CABLE CAN HOLD THOUSANDS OF FIBRES

LIGHT PULSES ARE CONVERTED BACK INTO ELECTRIC PULSES

YOU DO TALK NONSENSE, BETTY. THAT WOULD NEVER WORK!

A microphone turns the sound of your voice into electric pulses which are transformed into laser light signals. These whiz down the cable.

At the other end of the line the process is reversed and you hear sounds in your earhole.

And because light moves so fast and a laser can flicker at billions of times a second an optical fibre can carry a conversation down the line in the blink of an eye. And what's more, you can squash thousands of fibres in a single cable.

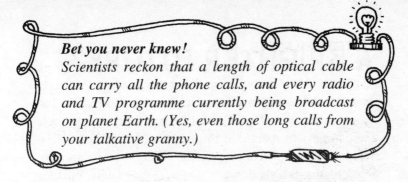

Bet you never knew!
Scientists reckon that a length of optical cable can carry all the phone calls, and every radio and TV programme currently being broadcast on planet Earth. (Yes, even those long calls from your talkative granny.)

And yet the wonders of optical fibres look pale compared with future developments. But is the future bright with promise or is it dark and frightening? Let's gaze into the crystal ball...

A BRIGHTER FUTURE?

Imagine there was no light on planet Earth except for your pocket torch. People would grope their way through the darkness to marvel at this amazing brightness. They would wonder at its beauty and its ability to turn darkness into colours and shadows.

WE PRAISE YOU MISTRESS OF THE LIGHT. YOU SHINE YOUR WONDROUS BEAM ON OUR HUMBLE FACES

But light is everywhere. And because we see it every day we don't think too much about it. What a pity.

Light is awesome, unbelievable, fantastic. And although the science of light seems frightening at first – the more you discover the more magical it seems. It's incredible that a humble light bulb makes photons and that these astonishing blips of energy can light up the sky in the day and at night you can see stars because their photons have travelled for millions of years to reach you.

It's even more astonishing to think that it's photons that give colour to a daffodil or power to a laser. And it's gobsmacking to peer in a mirror and know that you can only see yourself because every second billions of photons are bouncing off the mirror to create an image made of light.

But the latest discoveries of physicists are even MORE exciting, even more brain-boggling. And they're about to light up our future in totally unexpected ways. For example…

1 CREATIVE CHEMICAL CHAOS

In the 2000's scientists learnt how to use lasers to trigger chemical reactions. Traditionally, you had to heat things up over a grotty old Bunsen burner like the sort you find in schools.

But by using laser pulses of exactly the right length scientists can break chemicals into smaller groups of atoms to create brand new chemicals. And this could turn every industry that uses chemical reactions upside down.

2 SMALL IS BEAUTIFUL

Nowadays people can make a fibre optic cable thousands of times finer than the eye of a needle. And tiny lasers are possible too. In 1989 IBM made a laser one-tenth the thickness of a human hair. With a bit of careful packing you could fit a *million* of them into this box.

The laser was made from tiny crystals and this technology will make possible micro-holograms and tiny surgical instruments for delicate operations. In fact, miniature versions of any machine that uses a laser.

3 MARVELS IN STORE

By the 2000's, scientists had figured out how to stop and store light. At first this involved cooling atoms to ultra-cold temperature and trapping photons with lasers and magnets. But in 2005 scientists found that a purple substance made by slimy microbes could slow light too.

4 STRANGE LIGHT SIGNALS

By the 2000's scientists were experimenting with a brain-boggling effect called quantum entanglement. If you make a pair of photons, they behave as if they're in contact, even when they're hundreds of kilometres apart. You could even use this pair of freaky photons to send coded signals. And just imagine – you could combine tiny lasers and light storage and secrete photon codes to create something that makes a super computer like something your baby brother plays with…

5 THE ULTIMATE DREAM MACHINE

I'm talking about a computer that does billions of sums at the speed of light using photons to send information. And scientists are dreaming of such a machine – a machine so powerful that it could do all your maths homework for the next ten years in one-millionth of a second. Now that's progress for you!

Sure, light is the fastest moving thing in the universe. But science is beginning to catch up. The future's looking horribly bright – and that's the brilliant truth!

THE END

FRIGHTENING LiGHT QUIZ

Now find out if you're a **Frightening Light** expert!

Light up your life!

So, have you been switched on during this lightning journey through light? Are you a bright spark or still in the dark? Take this quick quiz and find out...

1 What are the two main ingredients of a rainbow?
a) Sunlight and a pot of gold
b) Sunlight and rain
c) Sunlight and oxygen

2 What mysteriously occurs when a photon hits an atom?
a) All its energy is absorbed and, exhausted, it disappears
b) It has so much energy that it splits the atom into a million pieces
c) The photon's energy can glue atoms together

3 How long does it take speedy sunlight to reach the Earth?
a) About the time it takes for you to sneeze and wipe the snot on your sleeve during your Science lesson (8.5 seconds)
b) About the time it takes for you to nod off in your Science lesson (8.5 minutes)
c) About the time it takes for you to zoom out of the door at the end of your Science lesson (8.5 milliseconds)

4 How many light waves could stretch across the dot at the bottom of this question mark?
a) Hundreds

b) 4,677 precisely

c) About five

5 Which of the following would make an atom spit out a photon?

a) Asking it nicely

b) Sticking it in the freezer

c) Popping it in the oven

6 What happens to a stream of light when it moves from air into water?

a) It bends, or refracts

b) It bounces back, or reflects

c) It starts doing backstroke

7 Why is the sky blue?

a) Because there are more blue light waves than there are other colours

b) Because more blue light photons are scattered by the air

c) Because light is reflected off the water that covers 70 per cent of the Earth's surface

8 If a plant reflects green light and absorbs all the other colours, what colour light does a banana reflect?

a) Yellow

b) All colours except yellow

c) Red and green

Answers
1b; 2a; 3b; 4a; 5c; 6a; 7b; 8c

Meet the scientists...

We'd still be living in the dark ages when it comes to light if it wasn't for a few freaky physicists who looked at light in a different way (often nearly blinding themselves in the process!). Can you match the discoveries below with the spectacular scientists responsible?

1 This freaky English physicist used a triangular lump of glass to prove that sunlight was made up of lots of different colours.

2 This German genius suggested that light came in the form of packets that he gave the curious name of 'quanta'.

3 This Dutch daredevil shed light on the mysteries of space by inventing the telescope.

BEAM ME UP, SCOTTY!

4 This mad-haired German-born scientist befuddled everyone by proving that light is both a wave and a particle (eh?!).

5 This ingenious American inventor set the world alight with his light bulb.

6 This famous French physicist found a way of measuring the speed of light using a spinning wheel and a mirror!

7 This amazing Arab scientist discovered that light is given out by glowing objects and that it always reflects at a predictable angle.

8 This energetic Englishman wowed the world with his discovery that light travels in weird waves.

a) Thomas Young
b) Armand Fizeau
c) Thomas Edison
d) Isaac Newton
e) Ibn al-Haytham
f) Hans Lippershay
g) Max Planck
h) Albert Einstein

Answers
1d; 2g; 3f; 4h; 5c; 6b 7e; 8a

What does it all mean?

These strange scientists used many weird and wonderful words to describe the ways light behaves and the objects it interacts with. Look at the list of words below – can you remember what on Earth they all mean?

1 Transparent
2 Reflection
3 Frequency
4 Interference
5 Refraction
6 Opaque
7 Diffraction
8 Translucent

a) The bizarre bending of light as it passes from one material to another.
b) The strange spreading out of light waves after they've passed through a small slit.
c) The name for an object that can block light and cast a spooky shadow.

d) The name for a frosty object that isn't so solid no

light can get through … but isn't completely see-through, either.

e) The bouncing back of light when it hits an object.

f) The name for something that has a thin layer of regularly spaced atoms which means lots of light can pass through.

g) The mysterious meeting of light waves when they make a brighter light or block each other out completely.

h) The number of times a weird wave of light wiggles each second.

Answers
1f; 2e; 3h; 4g; 5a; 6c; 7b; 8d

Light fantastic

Light is so amazing that you simply won't believe some of the things people say about it. Have a look at these fantastical statements and see if you can figure out which are strange but true and which are just strange…

1 You are only able to see your annoying little brother because light waves are bouncing off him.

2 Light is so brilliant it can even bend around corners.

3 Sunlight is made up of seven colours – red, orange, yellow, green, blue, indigo and violet.

4 Eating carrots helps you to see in the dark.

5 All the light on Earth comes from the sun – without our super star we'd all die in the darkness.

6 Stars seem to twinkle because the light from them is being bent by eerie gusts of wind.

7 People who are colour blind only see things in black and white.

8 Light is faster than anything, anywhere, ever…

Answers:

1 TRUE. You'd probably rather be left in the dark…

2 TRUE (AND FALSE). Ha ha! Trick question. Light waves can only travel in straight lines, but amazing scientists have invented things called optical fibres that can carry light round corners.

3 FALSE. Sunlight is made up of these seven colours and everything in between (and others on either side, actually). It's just that we only have specific words to describe seven of them.

4 FALSE. That's just a load of carroty cobblers. If you want to see in the dark, use a torch!

5 FALSE. Light can come from lots of other things – candles, your toaster, even curious creatures like fireflies. But we'd still all die if the sun stopped shining because sunlight is what helps plants grow, which keep us alive (but that's a whole other Horrible Science book…).

6 TRUE. Starlight moves in a straight line, like all other light, but it can be refracted by wild winds.

7 FALSE. People who are colour blind can usually distinguish some colours but not others.

8 TRUE. Nothing in the whole universe can travel faster than light.

Awesome eyesight

Without your amazing eyes you'd be completely in the dark. These miraculous machines take in light, figure out colours and form an image in your brain. So, let the light waves bounce off the page and use the clues to answer these curious questions about sight.

1 Which bit of your bulging eyeball lets in light? (CLUE: It may be the class swot)

2 What's the matter with you if you have mysterious myopia? (CLUE: You'll have to look closely to answer this one)

3 What happens to an object if you look at it through a concave lens? (CLUE: This is just a tiny clue)

4 What happens to your peculiar pupils when it gets dark? (CLUE: Oh – open your eyes!)

5 Which part of your awesome eye bends the light so you see things in focus? (CLUE: It sounds corny, but it's true)

6 If an object reflects all types of light, what colour do your eyes see it as? (CLUE: You know the answer, all white)

7 Which little bits on your retina allow you to see things in glorious Technicolour? (CLUE: You wouldn't want to put you ice cream in them, though)

8 What kind of lens makes an object look bigger? (CLUE: It's not complex)

Answers:
1 The pupil
2 You are short-sighted
3 It looks smaller
4 They get bigger to let in more light
5 The cornea
6 White
7 Cones
8 Convex

GULP!

HORRIBLE INDEX

accommodation (focuses light) 52–3
after-images 137
Alpha Centauri (our starry neighbour) 71
Andromeda galaxy, far, far away 71
angles of reflection 103
angles of refraction 122
arc-lights, dangerous 80–1
Archimedes (Greek scientist) 95
argon (gas) 90
astigmatism (eye problem) 118
astronomers, artful 23, 25–6, 28, 37, 64, 71–4, 92, 122
atoms, amazing 8, 17, 20, 22, 59, 73, 79, 81–2, 94, 100, 107, 110, 114, 126, 131–3, 139, 141–2, 146, 155–6
Ayrton, W.E. (British physicist) 98

bacteria, billions of 73, 76
bananas 128
bar codes 147
Basov, Nikolai (Russian scientist) 144
beeswax 80
Bell, Alexander Graham (American inventor) 143
binoculars 117
bioluminescence, brilliant 73
black 125, 129, 135–7
blindness 8, 56, 63, 81, 92

blood, black 129
bloodshot eyes 47
blue 8, 128, 130–7, 139–41
bottoms, glowing 77
Bradley, James (British astronomer) 28
brains, busy 42–3, 134, 137
Brocken Mountain, ghosts on 10, 12, 68
Bunsen burners, blasted 155

cameras 117
candles 12, 35, 79–80
canes, cruel 41
carbon dioxide (gas) 59
carbon filaments, in light bulbs 85, 88–9
cataracts (fluid in lens) 57, 63
cats 13, 136
CDs 148, 152
cells (body blobs) 44–6, 50, 63, 72, 76, 93, 136–7, 141
chemistry, chaotic 35, 47, 155
chromatic aberration (telescopic problem) 121–2
ciliary muscles (eyeball bits) 44, 53
clouds 92–3
black holes 92–3
codes 147, 156
coins, disappearing 112–3
colour deficiency 139–41
colours, crucial 15, 20, 32–4, 38–9, 46–7, 71–2, 114, 122–41, 154
comb jellies (glowing creatures) 76
computers 146–7, 156–7

169

concave lenses/mirrors (curve inwards) 104, 115, 117, 120, 122
concerts 149
cone cells (eyeball bits) 44, 46, 50, 136–7, 141
contact lenses 8, 120
convex lenses/mirrors (curve outwards) 105, 115–6, 118–9, 121
Coolidge, William (American inventor) 90
copepods (luminous plankton) 77
cornea (eyeball bit) 45–6, 51–3, 115, 118
credit cards 150
cross-eyed people, uncoordinated 47
crying 45, 54
crystals 93, 98, 156

Dalton, John (British chemist) 139–40
Davy, Humphrey (British scientist) 80
De la Rue, Warren (British photographer) 64–8
deep sea angler fish (glowing fish) 76
defence systems 145
deserts, dry 112
diffraction (light waves spreading out) 39
dinoflagellates (luminous plants) 77

earthquakes, measuring 149
eclipses, eerie 60–8
Edison, Thomas (American inventor) 82–9
Egyptians, awesome 95
Einstein, Albert (German scientist) 24, 40–3
Einstein, Hans (son of Albert) 42
Einstein, Mileva (wife of Albert/mathematician) 42
electricity 24, 80–3, 85, 87, 90, 114, 148, 150, 152

electromagnetism 8, 20
electrons, energetic 20, 82
endoscopes (look inside bodies) 93, 148
experiments, exciting 21–4, 29, 34, 37–8, 40, 47–8, 62–3, 69–71, 81, 100, 102–8, 112–13, 127, 136–9
expulsion 41
eyeballs, bulging 8, 25, 43–57, 92–3, 103, 116–20, 122, 128, 131, 136–41, 148
eyebrows 100
eyelashes 45

fact files, frightening 12, 94, 109, 125
factories 147
Fick, Adolf (German inventor) 120
films, for cameras 134
filters 134
fire flies (glowing beetles) 77
fish tanks, light-bending 109–10
Fizeau, Armand (French physicist) 28–9
flares, fiery 65, 68
fluorescent lights, flickering 82
focus 51, 53–4, 115, 118–20, 122–3
forces, fatal 24, 29
frequency (energy levels) 20, 125
Fresnel, Augustin Jean (French physicist) 39
future trends 154–7

galaxies, great 71
Galileo Galilei (Italian scientist) 26–8
gamma rays, deadly 20
gaslight 81
germs, gruesome 78, 138
ghosts, no such thing as 8, 10–2, 68, 106–7, 114, 143
glasses, wearing 117–20
glaucoma (gloop in eyeball) 56
glow, ghastly 12, 73, 75–9
glow-worms (beetles) 77
goggles 63, 93

170

Gould, Gordon (American scientist) 144
gravity, groovy 29
green 125, 128, 134–7, 140–1

halos 55, 122–3
heat 12, 15, 20, 24, 40, 80–1, 83, 96, 147
Herschel, John (British astronomer) 64–8
historians, horrible 102
holograms 150, 156
Hooke, Robert (British scientist) 34–36
horizon, horizontal 112
hospitals 25
Huygens, Christiaan (Dutch astronomer) 37, 39
hyperopia (long-sightedness) 118

Ibn al-Haytham, Abu al-Hassan (Arab scientist) 100–3
illusions, illusory 48
infections, unnecessary 138–9
interference (meeting of light waves) 39
Invisible Man 114–5, 126
iris (eyeball bit) 44, 56

Jannsen, Zacharius (Dutch inventor) 120

keratometers (eyeball-curve measurers) 120
Kruesli, John (Edison's assistant) 84

Langmuir, Irving (American inventor) 90
lasers, blistering 8, 29, 141–54, 156
Leavitt, Henrietta (American astronomer) 72
legs, short and stumpy 111
lenses, in eyeballs 45, 47, 50–1, 53, 57
lenses, made of glass 115–22, 150
Liebig, Justus von (German chemist) 96
light bulbs, brilliant 7, 13, 20, 58, 79, 82–91, 154
light waves 7, 16–7, 20, 37–40, 125
lighthouses 81, 90
Lindsay, James Bowman (Scottish inventor) 89
Lippershey, Hans (Dutch inventor) 120–21
long-sighted people 118–9
luciferin (glowing chemical) 73

Mackenzie, J.V. (Edison's assistant) 84–5
magnification 16, 116
Maiman, Theodore (American physicist) 144
matter, made of 17
Maxwell, James Clerk (Scottish physicist) 134, 140
mercury, uses for 81–2, 96
methane (gas) 78
Michelson, Albert (American scientist) 29
microbes, slimy 156
microscopes 16, 36, 109, 117, 120
mirages 92–3, 112
mirrors, murderous 14–5, 19, 28–9, 63, 91–3, 95–8, 100, 104–8, 115, 122–3, 145–6, 150, 154–5
missiles, shooting down 145, 147
mixing colours 134–6
moon, magic 14–5, 18, 60–2, 65–8, 73, 151
Murdock, William (Scottish inventor) 81
music 34, 148–9
myopia (short-sightedness) 118

Newton, Isaac (British scientist) 24, 29–36, 39, 122–3, 137–9
Nicholas of Cusa (German

churchman) 119
Nichols prisms 132
Nobel Prizes 133, 144
nuclear explosions 57

observatories 25
ophthalmologists (eyeball doctors) 25, 52, 118
ophthalmoscopes (look at eyeballs) 93
optic nerves (eyeball bits) 44, 56
optical fibres 93–4, 148, 152–3, 156
optical physicists (light scientists) 24
opticians (eyeball testers) 120
optics 24, 102–3
oxygen (gas) 46, 73, 78

paraffin candles, hazardous 80
patents 88, 144
Perry, J. (British physicist) 98
phones 151–3
phonographs (record players) 83
phosphor/phosphorus (glowing chemical) 79, 82
photography 134–5
photons, frightening 8, 16–20, 22–3, 26, 40, 47, 50, 59, 63, 71–2, 79, 82, 94–5, 100, 110, 131–3, 143, 145–6, 154–7
physicists, forceful 24, 39–40, 98, 144, 155
pigments (colour chemicals) 47, 114–5, 126
plague, bubonic 31, 35
Planck, Max (German physicist) 39–40
plankton, luminous 77
printers 150
prisms, pesky 30, 32–5, 123, 132
Prokhorov, Alexander (Russian scientist) 144
pupils (eyeball bits) 46, 49, 51

quanta (energy blips) 39–40
quantum electrodynamics (photon-swaps) 100
quantum entanglement, spooky 156

radio waves 20, 142–3
rainbows, ravishing 14–5, 32–4, 125
Raman, Chandrasejhara Vankata (Indian scientist) 129–33
random deviation 8
rattlesnakes, poisonous 14–5
red 20, 34, 126–9, 132, 134–7, 139–41, 146
reflections (bouncing light) 15, 22, 25, 39, 49, 63, 91–108, 113, 120, 123, 125, 127–9, 131–3, 135, 146, 148
refraction (bending light) 23, 33, 39, 47, 51, 53, 57, 73, 93, 109–15, 122, 137
relativity theories, revolutionary 40
retina (eyeball bit) 44, 46–7, 115, 118–20, 122, 136–7, 140, 148
road signs 92–3
rods (eyeball bits) 44, 46, 50, 52–3, 55–6, 63, 72
Roemer, Ole (Danish astronomer) 28
Romans, rotten 95
Royal Society (top science club) 34

scanners 147
Schawlow, Arthur (American scientist) 143
scientists, bright 7, 23–43, 50–1, 78, 82, 93, 95, 97–8, 100–3, 105, 115, 129–32, 136–40, 142, 144, 150–1, 153, 156–7
sclera (eyeball bit) 45
scrying (fortune-telling) 98
sea 130–3
Secchi, Angelo (Spanish scientist) 68

172

seeing double 56–7
shadows, sinister 12, 60, 63, 66, 68–70, 87, 127, 154
sheepskin, glowing 82
shellfish 92–3
shoes, shiny 99
short-sighted people 118–20
signals, speedy 151–2, 156
sky 8, 13, 112, 130–3, 154
snow blindness 92–3
sodium, uses for 81, 129
space 40
spectres 12, 68
spectroscopes (colour-studying instruments) 123
speed of light 24, 26–9, 110, 157
spiders, hairy 116–7
squid 136
staring, dangers of 63
stars, super 13, 25, 44, 58–9, 62, 66, 71–3, 154
street lights 81, 129
strip lights 82
Strutt, John (British scientist) 129–32
Strutt, Robert (John's son) 132–3
sun, swallowed 61–2, 66–8
sunlight/sunshine, sizzling 7, 12–15, 32–4, 57–74
sunsets 124, 131
Swan, Joseph (British inventor) 82, 88–9
swimming pools, light-bending 110–1

tallow candles, stinking 80
telescopes, traditional 28, 36, 109, 117, 120–2
television 92–3, 153
Thucydides (Greek writer) 61
time 40
toasters 20
toilets, glowing 77
tomatoes, tasty 126–7
toothpicks, in eyes 138

Townes, Charles (American scientist) 142–3
transparent (see-through) things 126
tungsten filaments 90

ultraviolet light 20, 82
university laboratories 24

Venetians, top secret 96
violet 20, 136, 140
vision 136–41

wavelengths, wiggly 8, 123
welding 148
Wells, H.G. (British writer) 115
white light 125–6, 135, 137
whites of eyes 47
wicks, wicked 80
will o' the wisps 78

X-ray fish 126

yellow 128, 136–7
Young, Thomas (British scientist) 36–9, 50, 140

173

SOUNDS DREADFUL

INTRODUCTION

Listen to this…
The younger you are, the LOUDER you are. Babies love making noise…

RATTLE! WAAAGH! WAAAGH! RATTLE! RATTLE! WAAAGH! WAAAGH!

And so do kids…

I CAN YELL LOUDER THAN YOU

BET YOU CAN'T!

And teenagers think really loud music is **brilliant!**

BLAST BOOM

TURN THAT THING OFF!

But as people grow older they change. They settle down

and quieten down. Your parents no longer think LOUD is good. They think that anything LOUD sounds dreadful. Especially loud sounds made by YOU!

So you'd better read this book q-u-i-e-t-l-y. And guess what? Teachers are *even* worse.

In fact, the only sound teachers seem to enjoy is the sound of their own voices. Sounding off about boring things. Like science, for example. And just to put you off the idea of making noise – teachers teach you about sound in science.

Sounds dreadful, doesn't it? But it doesn't have to be…

Listen to a few more exciting sound facts and see if they make your ears prick up:

• A single note can shatter glass.

• Sound makes your eyeballs shiver in their sockets.

• Sound stuns and even kills people.

And that's not all. This book is full of facts about a world of dreadful sounds – from bells that can burst your blood vessels, to sinister sound guns that can make you dash for the toilet. Read all about it and afterwards you can sound off in science class to your heart's content. You're bound to get a good hearing.

And who knows? You could become a big noise in science. One thing's for sure – the world will never sound the same to you again. So now that you're all ears, just turn the page…

SOUNDING OFF

What do the following have in common?

a) Your pet mouse.

b) Your science teacher.

c) A 60-piece orchestra.

Give up? No, the answer *isn't* that they all eat cheese. The correct answer is they all use *sound* to grab your attention. The orchestra needs sound to play a symphony, the mouse needs sound to squeak and your science teacher … well, just imagine there was no such thing as sound. You couldn't listen to a boring science lesson. And she'd never get to tell you off. That would be tragic!

For animals sound is equally vital because, just like us, animals use sound to pass on vital messages. Just imagine what would happen if your dog couldn't whimper when it was time to go out for "walkies". You might forget to take him out…

SPEAK LIKE A SCIENTIST

Scientists have their very own language which only they understand. Now's your chance to learn a few key words.

And afterwards you can sound off and amaze your friends and silence your teacher with your word-power.

Enormous AMPLITUDE (am-plee-tude)
This means how loud a sound is. Stronger sound waves mean louder sounds, or greater amplitude. The word amplitude comes from "ample" which also means BIG.

Fantastic FREQUENCY
Frequency means the number of vibrations a second that make up a sound (a vibration is the scientific name for a wobble). These can be ear-bogglingly fast – for example bats can squeak at over 100,000 vibrations a second. Higher frequency means that the sound is higher, which is why bats squeak rather than growl. By the way, frequency is measured in hertz, (pronounced hurts and written Hz). So higher frequency makes more hertz.

Tuneful TONES
No, this has nothing to do with keeping in tone by physical exercise. A tone is a sound with just one frequency (just to confuse you, most sounds have lots all

mixed up). You can make a tone by hitting a special tool called a tuning fork on a smooth surface.

Rumbling RESONANCE (rez-o-nance)

This is when vibrations hit an object at a certain frequency. These make the object wobble too. The vibrations get stronger and stronger and the sound gets louder and louder. Until it can sound really deafening. (See page 200 for more details.)

Happenin' HARMONICS

Imagine plucking a guitar string. The string vibrates in several ways to make one main tone and several lesser ones. Harmonics are the lesser tones that help to make your playing sound tuneful. And if it isn't, your music teacher is going to get a hammering headache.

Got all that? That'll give you something to shout about in your next science lesson. But here's something you can make an even bigger noise about. Just imagine what it would be like if YOU became a real-life pop star…

Now's your chance…

COULD YOU BE A POP STAR?

You don't need too many qualifications to be a pop star. Although talent helps, it doesn't seem too vital. Just so long as you actually enjoy music and dancing YOU could be the latest hottest biggest new pop sensation. But you'll need to be ready to record your first hit single. To find out how, read on.

To show us the technical side of the business we've hired (at great expense) top DJ and record producer Jez Liznin. And to help explain the vital background facts about sound that any budding pop star needs to know we've recruited scientist, Wanda Wye.

YO WANDA! INTERESTED IN COOL MUSIC?

SLAP!

ER YES - BUT I'M ALSO INTERESTED IN SOUND SCIENCE

STEP ONE: SOUND SYSTEMS
Silent soundproofing

When you record a hit record you don't want to pick up the sound of next door's TV. Jez's sound studio is lined with a thick hi-tech sound insulator to keep out unwanted noises.

OK, it's only cardboard egg boxes behind plasterboard.

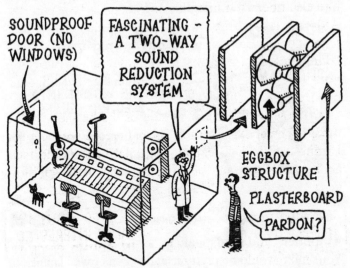

SOUNDPROOF DOOR (NO WINDOWS)

FASCINATING – A TWO-WAY SOUND REDUCTION SYSTEM

EGGBOX STRUCTURE

PLASTERBOARD

PARDON?

The soft cardboard soaks up the vibes like a nice comfy pillow. And they get lost in there, which is why it's so quiet in the studio. Except when Jez opens his big mouth.

Mighty microphone

This is what you'll need to sing or play instruments into. You'll need to get quite close to it, so you can call it mike for short.

HERE'S THE MIKE

AMAZING! AN ACOUSTO-ELECTRIC TRANSDUCER

AND HERE'S MIKE THE STUDIO CAT

What Wanda means is that the microphone turns sound into electric pulses. Like this…

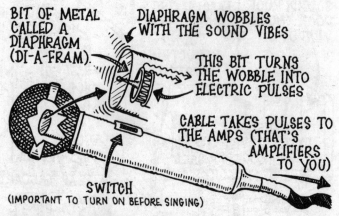

BIT OF METAL CALLED A DIAPHRAGM (DI-A-FRAM)

DIAPHRAGM WOBBLES WITH THE SOUND VIBES

THIS BIT TURNS THE WOBBLE INTO ELECTRIC PULSES

CABLE TAKES PULSES TO THE AMPS (THAT'S AMPLIFIERS TO YOU)

SWITCH
(IMPORTANT TO TURN ON BEFORE SINGING)

Amplifiers and loudspeakers

Your mike would be pretty useless on its own. Thanks to the mike, the sound of your fabulous singing is now in the form of electrical pulses. And you can't listen to pulses, can you? Well, you could but it would be about as thrilling as listening to a hair dryer. So you need a loudspeaker to turn the pulses back into your own groovy tune. And an amplifier makes your tune loud enough to hear – sometimes a bit too loud.

186

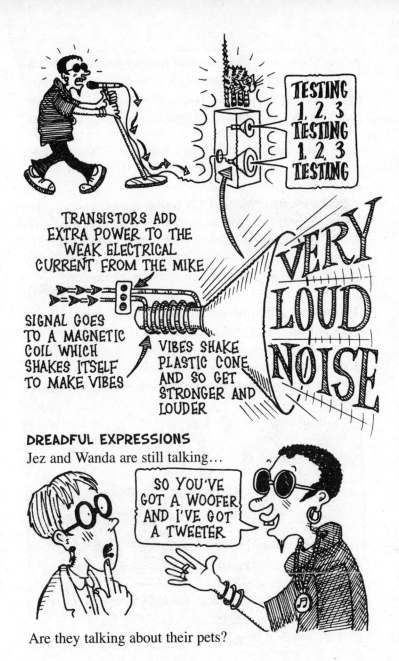

TESTING 1, 2, 3 TESTING 1, 2, 3 TESTING

TRANSISTORS ADD EXTRA POWER TO THE WEAK ELECTRICAL CURRENT FROM THE MIKE

SIGNAL GOES TO A MAGNETIC COIL WHICH SHAKES ITSELF TO MAKE VIBES

VIBES SHAKE PLASTIC CONE AND SO GET STRONGER AND LOUDER

VERY LOUD NOISE

DREADFUL EXPRESSIONS

Jez and Wanda are still talking…

SO YOU'VE GOT A WOOFER AND I'VE GOT A TWEETER

Are they talking about their pets?

Answer: No. They're talking about loudspeakers. A woofer is a loudspeaker that only plays low-pitched sounds. A tweeter is a loudspeaker that only plays (you guessed it) high-pitched sounds.

Still want to be a star? Jez and Wanda will be back later on to give you more sound advice.

DREADFUL ANIMAL SOUND QUIZ

Imagine that you are a small animal. What would you do in the following situations? Remember, your choice is a matter of life and death. Choose incorrectly and you might end up as a tasty snack for a larger creature.

1 You are a South American possum (poss-um – a small furry animal with a grasping tail that lives in trees) and you meet a Brazilian screaming frog. The frog screams (that's how it got its name, oddly enough). What do you do?

a) Eat the frog. It'll take more than a scary scream to put you off.
b) Run away – the frog is warning you that there's a dangerous animal nearby.
c) Back off. The frog is telling you it's poisonous to eat.

2 You're a North American ground squirrel. There's a rattlesnake in your burrow and it's after your babies. You can't see the snake but you can hear its sinister rattle. It sounds surprisingly high-pitched and slow. What do you do?

a) Run for it. The rattle warns you that the snake is big and poisonous. Yikes! The babies can fend for themselves.

b) The slow rattle means the snake is moving slowly. So you've got time to dig an escape tunnel for yourself and your babies.

c) Attack the snake. The rattle proves the snake is smaller than average and rather tired. So you might just win the fight.

3 You're a lapwing (a bird) living in a swamp. You hear a loud three-note call from a redshank (that's another type of bird). What do you do?

a) Go looking for fish. The cry tells you there's food nearby.

b) The call is a warning. There's a gang of crows in the way and they'd like to eat your babies (and the red shank's). You join a posse of other lapwings to fight the invaders off.
c) Nothing. The cry tells you rain's on the way and being a swamp bird you're not scared of a drop of water.

Bet you never knew!
Human beings also use sounds to communicate – so you knew that already? Well, bet you never knew that human voices can make more different sounds than any other mammal. That's because you can move your tongue and lips in many different ways to form lots of weird and wonderful sounds. Try making a few now...

Dare you discover ... sounds all around you?

You will need:

Yourself

One pair of ears (If you're lucky you may already have these. You should find them attached to the sides of your head.)

What you do:

1 Nothing

DELIGHTED TEACHER

ABSOLUTE SILENCE

I SHOULD TRY THIS MORE OFTEN

2 Sit very still and listen.

What did you notice?

a) Nothing. And it gets really boring after the first half hour.

b) I started hearing all kinds of sounds I hadn't noticed before.

c) I heard strange sounds from inside my body.

Answer: b) and possibly **c)**. Sounds are all around us. There are loads of everyday sounds that we don't take any notice of. Sounds like the neighbour's cat throwing up fur balls, your gran sucking a wine gum, or a sparrow with a bad cough. If there aren't any sounds going on, you can always listen to your own breathing. (If you're not breathing it might be a good idea to see a doctor.)

191

Sounds dreadful fact file

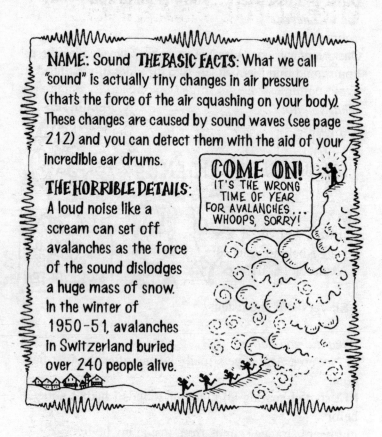

NAME: Sound **THE BASIC FACTS:** What we call "sound" is actually tiny changes in air pressure (that's the force of the air squashing on your body). These changes are caused by sound waves (see page 212) and you can detect them with the aid of your incredible ear drums.

THE HORRIBLE DETAILS: A loud noise like a scream can set off avalanches as the force of the sound dislodges a huge mass of snow. In the winter of 1950–51, avalanches in Switzerland buried over 240 people alive.

COME ON! IT'S THE WRONG TIME OF YEAR FOR AVALANCHES... WHOOPS, SORRY!

COME OVER 'EAR AND WE'LL READ THE NEXT CHAPTER

DREADFUL HEARING

Bats, humans and grasshoppers all have something in common. Ears. Most of the time you don't notice them. Well, not unless there's something dreadfully odd about them...

WHAT'RE YOU STARING AT?

But you'd soon notice if your own ears weren't working too well, and you'd certainly notice if you couldn't hear because behind your ears lies an amazing bit of natural engineering. Listen up.

DREADFUL EXPRESSIONS

Two doctors are at the theatre. But can they hear the play?

AAAAARGH!

WELL, MY AUDITORY OSSICLES ARE AGITATING MY OVAL WINDOWS

Is this painful?

Answer: Not usually. She means the bones in her ear have vibrated and passed on their motion to the "oval window" covering the entrance to her inner ear. So her answer could have been, "Yes". Confused yet? Just lend an ear to this.

193

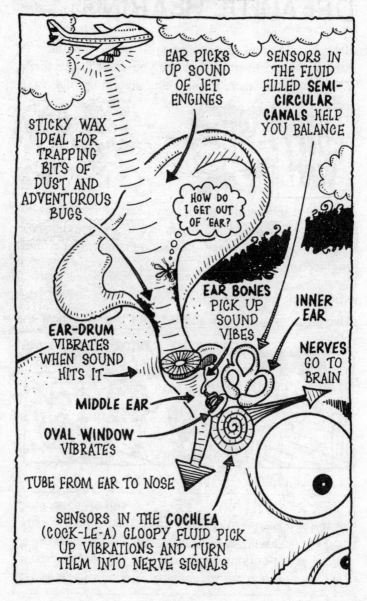

AND HERE'S THE EAR IN ACTION...

Imagine a wandering ugly bug, say a fly, sneaked into the ear. Here's what it would see.

1 The external ear canal (that's ear 'ole to you)

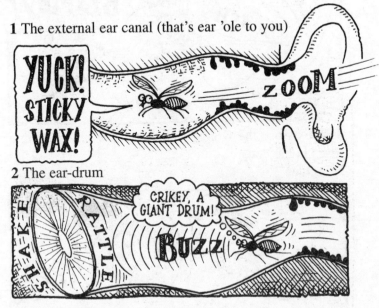

2 The ear-drum

3 Meanwhile, in the middle ear the ear bones are doing their castanets impression by passing on the fly's irritating buzz.

Can you see where the names came from?

4 The semi-circular canals

Scientists use the word "canal" to mean any long thin space in the body.

5 Cochlea

That fly's a genius. That's where the name comes from.

6 And the nerves are buzzing with sound messages for the brain.

COULD YOU BE A SCIENTIST?

Would you make a good sound scientist? Try to predict the results of these sound experiments. If you get them right you'll certainly have something to shout about.

1 Scientists have discovered that our hearing is sharpest for sounds of a certain frequency. Which sounds do we hear most clearly?

a) Loud music

b) A coin dropping on the floor

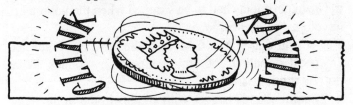

c) A teacher talking

2 Every musical instrument sounds a bit different even when they play the same note. Some make a smooth tinkling noise and some make more of a rattle or a blare. This is because of the unique pattern of sound vibrations

197

or timbre (tim-bruh) made by each instrument. Scientist Steve McAdams wanted to discover if people could spot these differences. What did he find?

a) People are useless at spotting sound differences. They said all the instruments sounded the same to them.

EASY! BUT THEN I USED TO PLAY THE RECORDER MYSELF

PARP

b) People are brilliant at this. They could tell the difference between the instruments even when Steve used a computer to take out almost all the timbre differences.

c) The experiments had to be stopped when the volunteers developed raging earache.

3 A scientist at Harvard Medical School, USA, studied electrical signals in the brain triggered by sounds. What do you think he found?

a) Tuneful sounds trigger wild signals in the brain.

b) All sounds trigger regular patterns of signals.

c) Tuneful sounds trigger regular patterns and dreadful clashing noises trigger wild signals.

AND THIS IS ME SINGING TUNEFULLY IN THE BATH...

Bet you never knew!
Diana Deutsch, Professor of Psychology at the University of California, USA, studied the way our ears hear different notes. She played different notes in each ear of a volunteer.

Amazingly, even when she played a high note in the left ear the volunteer said they heard the sound in their right ear. The experiment showed that your right ear "wants" to hear higher notes than the left ear. Sounds weird, doesn't it?

HORRIBLY HARD OF HEARING

But, of course, these sound experiments depend on one vital factor. Hearing. The volunteer had to hear the sounds in the first place, and some people can't.

Sounds dreadful fact file

NAME: Deafness

THE BASIC FACTS: About 16 per cent of people in Britain have less than perfect hearing. About one in twenty people have some difficulty in hearing conversation.

THE DREADFUL DETAILS:

1 Deafness can be caused by listening to loud music. This can destroy the nerve endings that join on to the cochlea. Better shout that to your noisy teenage brother or sister.

2 Disease can destroy hearing. Temporary deafness can occur when the middle ear gets infected and fills up with pus. Yuck!

3 As people get older the sensors in the cochlea die off. That's why you may have to shout in your gran's ear hole.

THANKS FOR THE NEW PYJAMAS, GRAN!

GO TO THE BAHAMAS? LOVELY, I'LL GO AND PACK!

HELPFUL HEARING AIDS

Nowadays deafness can be helped by hearing-aids or cochlea implants. A hearing-aid is a miniature microphone linked to an amplifier that makes sounds louder. A cochlea implant is a tiny radio receiver fitted under the skin that receives radio signals from an earpiece behind the ear. The implant then converts the signals to electrical pulses that trigger signals along the nerves to the brain. Brilliant, eh?

Bet you never knew!

In the USA, a man named Henry Koch complained of hearing music in his head. Tests showed that a tiny lump of carborundum (car-bor-run-dum), a hard black chemical from a dentist's drill, had stuck in his tooth. The crystals in the chemical were picking up and boosting the power of radio waves from a nearby transmitter. This triggered vibrations which the poor man heard as music.

But before the invention of modern hearing aids, in about 1900, people had to make do with this...

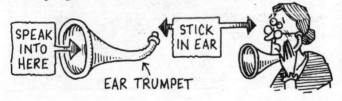

You shout into the ear trumpet. The vibrations can't escape from the trumpet except by passing into granny's lug hole. So your voice sounds louder.

But how would deafness affect a composer of music? A person for whom hearing is more important than anything else in the world. Someone like German composer Ludwig van Beethoven (1770–1827) for example.

HEARING IS BELIEVING

Some people called him a genius. Others called him crazy and sometimes even ruder things. His music was inspired by listening to country sounds, murmuring streams, storms and bird calls. He composed thrilling, dramatic melodies that mirrored his passionate feelings about life and art. Hearing had made him what he was.

But in 1800 Beethoven noticed a ringing in his ears and over the next twenty years his hearing failed. He was forced to try a weird variety of different-shaped ear trumpets. The deafness might have been caused by a disease of the bones in Beethoven's middle ear.

The treatments he took were useless:

• Cold baths in smelly river water.

• Pouring almond oil into his ear holes.

• Wearing strips of bark over his ears.

• Wearing painful plasters on his arms until he got blisters.

Beethoven couldn't hear people talking. Instead, he wrote his friends little notes and they wrote back to him.

He gave his nephew Karl piano lessons and boasted the boy was brilliant. (He must be, thought Beethoven, because he had the best teacher in the world.) It was lucky Beethoven couldn't hear the young boy's dreadful playing. Beethoven's deafness made him really miserable. He also began to pong because he rarely bothered to wash or change his clothes. He never brushed his hair. (Don't get any ideas from this – missing a bath doesn't make you a genius.)

Beethoven could no longer hear well enough to conduct his own music. Several concerts were dreadful flops because he conducted the orchestra too slowly.

But amazingly enough, deafness didn't harm Beethoven's work as a composer. Some experts think he even got better. He used to imagine how the music would sound. And he had a special trick that helped him "listen" to a piano.

Dare you discover ... how to "hear" like Beethoven?

You will need:

One 0.5 cm wide rubber band

One pair of teeth – preferably your own

WARNING DON'T LET GO OF RUBBER BAND, SUDDENLY!

What you do:

1 Stretch the rubber band between your fingers and twang it. Note how loud the sound is.

2 Put one end of the band between your teeth. Stretch the band. (Don't let go!) Twang it again.

What did you notice?

a) The twang sounded louder the first time.

b) The twang sounded louder the second time.

c) The twang sounded a higher note the second time.

Answer: b) The twang sounds louder because the sound vibrations pass directly to your inner ear via the bones in your skull. These are very good at passing on sound vibrations. Beethoven used a drumstick held in his teeth to feel sound vibrations from a piano in the same way.

But for some people life is even harder. Try to imagine what it's like to be completely blind and deaf. The world would be dark and silent. And if you were a baby how would you ever learn a thing? This was the challenge for Helen Keller (1880–1968) who was deaf and blind and didn't know how to talk. Here's how her teacher, Annie O'Sullivan might have told her story...

A TOUCH OF MAGIC

Boston, USA Spring 1927

The young reporter was in a hurry. He had a deadline to meet and the editor back at *The Daily Globe* office was getting impatient for his story.

"So, Annie, may I call you that? You were Helen's teacher for many years. But what was she really like?"

The old woman smiled weakly. "Well, she was very naughty when she was a young girl. She smashed her mum's plates and stuck her fingers in her dad's food. Then she'd pinch her grandma and chase her from the room."

The reporter raised an eyebrow and stopped scribbling in his notebook.

"So, the famous Helen Keller was a bit of a wild child? Our readers will be shocked."

"Helen couldn't hear or see after an illness that she'd had as a baby. She knew people talked using their lips and she wanted to join in. But she couldn't because she'd never learnt how to talk. So Helen got cross instead. She drove her parents crazy. Her uncle said she ought to be locked up somewhere."

The old woman took a sip of tea.

"So I bet Helen's parents were pleased when you turned up. You being a teacher of deaf children."

"Yes, they were! They'd written to my boss at the charity in desperation asking him to send someone and I got the job. But Helen was less impressed. I remember our first meeting like it was yesterday. I tried to give her a hug and she struggled like a wild cat."

The reporter tucked his pencil behind his ear.

"So the famous Helen Keller was like a wild cat," he smirked, "Bet you gave her a smack to keep her in line." The old lady looked shocked. Her saucer rattled as she replaced her cup.

"Oh no, that was never my way. I wanted Helen to be my friend as well as my pupil. Of course, I had to be firm sometimes..."

"Yeah, yeah," broke in the reporter, "but what our readers really want to know is how you taught her. I mean, it's not like she could hear or see anything."

"That was the big problem. All day long I tried to get Helen to understand me by tapping her hand. It was a special code – each letter of the alphabet was a certain number of taps. But Helen didn't understand. It was *so* frustrating."

"Don't suppose it meant anything to her seeing as she didn't know how to read or even what an alphabet was."

"Well, yes I know, but at the time I thought Helen would guess someone was trying to make contact. She'd already made up a few signs herself. Like when she wanted ice cream she'd pretend to shiver."

The reporter was drumming his fingers and fidgeting. "OK, Annie. So you had a problem. How did you get through to Helen in the end?"

"Don't be so fast, young man, I was coming to that. One day we were out for a walk and came across a woman pumping water. Well, I had a brainwave. I put Helen's hand under the stream, and I spelt out W-A-T-E-R by tapping on her hand. Helen twigged at once and then I knew what to do. I got Helen to feel or taste or smell things. For example, she learnt about the sea by paddling in the waves. Then I told her what they were by tapping. Yes, just like you're doing with your fingers."

The reporter stopped tapping as Annie continued...

"For Helen it was incredible, unbelievable. Just imagine it! You're locked in a totally dark and silent world for seven years, and then suddenly one day you realize that someone is actually trying to make contact with you. Helen changed as if by magic. She stopped being naughty and worked really hard."

The journalist checked his watch. Time was running short. He needed to spice up the story. A new angle.

"But Helen can talk now. What our readers want to know is how you managed to teach her."

"Helen knew things vibrate to make a sound. She could feel my throat move when I talked." Annie put her worn old fingers up to her thin neck. "We brought in a speech expert, Miss Fuller. By touching the teacher's throat and tongue and lips Helen found how they moved. Then she had a go herself.

"The first words Helen ever said were, 'I feel warm'. Well, she needed ten lessons just to get that far. But Helen stuck at it. And then..."

"You two went all over the world," interrupted the reporter as he buttoned his coat, "and Helen made grand speeches about the needs of people who can't see and hear." "Yes," the old lady agreed, "and we still live together. Thank goodness for our housekeeper Polly, she looks after Helen most of the time now as I'm

209

getting on a bit. Matter of fact, they're both out in town shopping at the moment."

The reporter stifled a yawn as the old lady continued.

"Mind you, Helen is very capable – despite everything. As I'm sure you've heard, Helen went to university and got a degree. It was all her own work, you know."

The reporter chewed his pencil impatiently. Then he gave a nasty little smile. He scented the new angle.

"It's an amazing story, Annie. But our readers have heard it all before. Devoted teacher helps little girl to discover the world. But maybe there's another side. What do you say to people who claim Helen wasn't that smart and you did the work for her?"

The old lady looked at the young man blankly, then her face filled with anger.

"Well, that's where you're wrong!" she declared fiercely. "It was Helen who did the learning. Yes, Helen is clever – but that's not the point! You see, I'm blind now myself. Never could see much, in fact. But I've come to realize that even if they can't see or hear, quite ordinary people can still do amazing things. Helen Keller taught me that."

The reporter felt stunned, but his mind was still fixed on the story. "Ordinary people can do amazing things…" *Hmm, I like that,* he thought as he closed his notebook. It would make a great opening line.

So that's hearing for you – tiny little air vibrations that rattle your ear bones. Sound waves seem pretty harmless, don't they? Well no, actually sound waves can be dreadful. They can smash windows and buildings and shake an entire aeroplane into little pieces. Now we're in for a bumpy ride, so fasten your seat belts and prepare for a bit of TURBULENCE.

SPEEDY SOUND WAVES

Let's have a nice big round of applause for this chapter. Notice anything? When you clap your hands, the noise you hear is a sound wave. Sound waves are happening all around you all the time.

They zoom outwards like the ripples on a pond when you chuck a rock into the middle. But not all sound waves are the same…

Sounds dreadful fact file

NAME: Sound waves

THE BASIC FACTS: A sound wave happens when clumps of atoms (scientists call them molecules) get shoved together and bump apart again. As they leap apart some molecules bump into others further away. So you get a wave of bumping molecules spreading out like a ripple on a pond.

THE DREADFUL DETAILS: It's not safe to stand next to a big bell when it rings. Powerful sound waves from the huge bell at Notre Dame Cathedral in Paris can burst blood vessels in your nose. Some visitors get nasty nose bleeds.

Scientists use an amazing machine called an oscilloscope (o-sill-oscope) to measure sound waves. The sound waves make a beam of electrons (tiny high energy bits) jump about on a screen.

Here's what a sound wave looks like…

A sound wave shows up as a curve or zigzag. The bigger the peak the greater the amplitude (loudness).

faster vibrations =
closer together peaks =
higher frequency =
higher pitch of sound

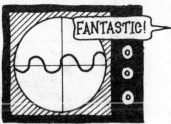

slower vibrations =
peaks further apart =
lower frequency =
lower pitch of sound

FANTASTIC FREQUENCY

Frequency is measured in Hertz (Hz) – that's vibrations per second, remember (see page 181). Your amazingly alert ears can pick up low-frequency sounds from about 25 vibrations per second, and they hear up to an ear-smacking 20,000 vibrations every second!

High-frequency sounds include…
• A mouse squeaking.

• A human squeaking after seeing the mouse.

• A bike chain in need of a drop of oil.

Low-frequency sounds include…
• A bear growling.

• Your dad growling in the morning.

• Your stomach growling before lunch.

Bet you never knew!
Small things vibrate faster. That's why they make higher-frequency sounds than big things. So that's why your voice sounds higher than your dad's, and a violin sounds more squeaky than a double bass.

As you grow up, the vocal chords in your throat that make sounds get bigger. So your voice gets deeper.

Dare you discover … how to see sound waves?

You will need:
A torch
A large piece of cling film
A cake tin without a base
A large elastic band
Sellotape
A piece of kitchen foil

What you do:
1 Stretch the clingfilm tightly over one end of the cake tin. Secure the clingfilm using the elastic band as shown.
2 Use the sellotape to stick the piece of foil off-centre on the clingfilm as shown.

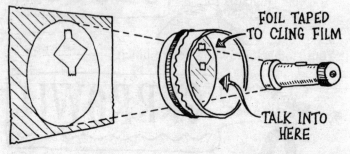

FOIL TAPED TO CLING FILM

TALK INTO HERE

3 Darken the room.
4 Place the torch on a table and angle it so the light reflects from the piece of foil on to the wall.
5 Talk into the open end of the cake tin.

What do you notice about the reflection?
a) It jumps around.
b) It stays rock steady.
c) The reflection gets brighter or dimmer depending on how loud your voice is.

TEST YOUR TEACHER

Here's your chance to sound your teacher out. Ask your teacher to say whether they think each answer is TRUE or FALSE, and here comes the tricky bit – ask them to explain *why*.

Important note: there are two marks for each correct answer. But your teacher is only allowed one mark if they only get the TRUE/FALSE bit right.

1 You can listen to a concert underwater even if you're at the other end of the swimming pool. TRUE/FALSE

2 You can use sound to count the number of times a fly flaps its wings in a second. TRUE/FALSE

3 You can hear sounds more quickly on a hot day. TRUE/FALSE

4 If you lived in a lead box you wouldn't be able to hear any sounds from the outside. TRUE/FALSE

Answers: 1 TRUE. Sound travels easily through water. That's why you can hear a rubber band twang even when you hold it underwater. Sound waves pass through water molecules in the same way as air molecules. But the concert would sound muffled because the water would press into your ears and stop your eardrums vibrating normally. (You could make this a trick question and say FALSE because no one can hold their breath that long.) **2 TRUE.** Scientists know the number of vibrations per second for each musical note. All they have to do is to find a note that sounds the same as the beating of a fly's wing. The wing will beat at the same speed. Using this technique scientists have found that a housefly's wings can beat over 200 times a second. **3 TRUE.** When air is warmer the molecules have more energy and move faster. But sound only travels about 3 per cent faster so you probably won't notice the difference. **4 FALSE.** Sound passes easily through solid metal. But it does pass more slowly through lead compared with steel – 4,319 km per hour (2,684 mph), compared to 18,111 km per hour (11,254 mph). But you can still hear the sound clearly.

WHAT YOUR TEACHER'S SCORE MEANS…

Score 7–8 points. This means EITHER

a) Your teacher is a genius. He/she is wasted as a teacher. We're dealing with Nobel Prize winning material here. OR

b) (More likely) they've read this book. In which case disqualify them for cheating.

Score 5–6 points. Fair but could do better. About average for a teacher.

Score 1–4 points. Your teacher may sound knowledgeable but they need to do **a lot more homework**.

COULD YOU BE A SCIENTIST?

One of the most amazing sound effects was discovered by an Austrian scientist called Christian Doppler (1803–1853). But in 1835 young Christian was desperate, dejected and departing. He couldn't find a job. So he sold all his belongings and got ready to set off for America.

At the last minute, a letter arrived offering him a job as Professor of Mathematics at Prague University (now in the Czech Republic). This was a stroke of luck because it was here that Doppler discovered what became known as the Doppler effect.

Doppler reckoned that when a moving sound passes it always changes pitch in the same way – that's the Doppler effect. As the sound waves come towards you they're squashed together. So you hear them in quick succession at a higher frequency. As the sound moves away you hear it at a lower frequency because the sound waves are more widely spaced.

To test Doppler's weird idea a Dutch scientist called Christoph Buys Ballot (1817–1890) filled a train carriage with buglers and listened as they whizzed past him. What do you think he heard?

Clue: the test proved Doppler was right.

a) As the buglers came closer the sound grew higher. As they moved away the sound got lower.

b) As the buglers came closer the sound grew lower. As they moved away the sound got higher.

c) The buglers were out of tune and the roar of the train almost drowned them out.

Answer:
a) Higher-frequency sound waves = higher sounds, remember? If you stand by a busy road and listen to cars going past you can hear the Doppler effect for yourself. Award yourself half a mark if your answer was c). These problems did happen but not badly enough to spoil the experiment.

SUPERSONIC SOUND SCIENTISTS

Have you ever watched a distant firework display? Ever wondered why you see the lovely coloured sparks but don't hear the bangs until a moment or two later?

It proves light travels faster than sound. But how fast does sound travel? A French priest called Marin Mersenne (1588–1648) had a brilliant plan to check it out.

He got a friend to fire a cannon. Marin stood a distance away and timed the gap between the flash when the gun was fired and the bang when the sound waves reached him.

But he didn't have an accurate clock so he counted his heartbeats instead.

In fact, he didn't do too badly. After scientists measured the speed of sound accurately they realized Marin's figure, 450 metres per second was a bit fast. But maybe Marin got excited and his heart speeded up.

One cold day in 1788, two French scientists fired two cannon 18 km apart. The second cannon provided a double check on the first and the distance between the two was about as far as each scientist could see with a telescope. They counted the time between the flashes and the bangs.

But what scientists really needed was a bit of posh equipment to make a more accurate measurement. And that's why French scientist Henri Regnault (1810–1878) built this ingenious sound machine. But would it work – or was it just a long shot?

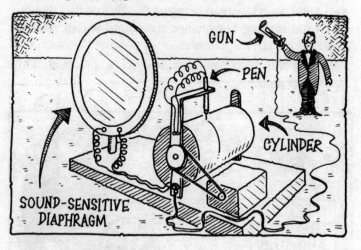

GUN

PEN

CYLINDER

SOUND-SENSITIVE DIAPHRAGM

HERE'S WHAT HAPPENED...

1 The cylinder went round at a regular speed and the pen made a line.

2 The pen was controlled by two electric circuits.

3 When the gun fired the circuit was broken and the pen-line jumped to a new position. I suppose that's what you call "jumping the gun". Ha, ha!

4 When the diaphragm picked up the sound, the circuit was restored and the pen flicked back to its original position.

Regnault knew how fast the cylinder was turning. So he measured the marks made by the pen and this told him how quickly the test had happened. His measurements proved sound travels at 1,220 km per hour (760 mph).

But despite Regnault's hard work the measure for the speed of sound is named after a completely different scientist.

Hall of fame: Ernst Mach (1835–1916)
Nationality: Austrian

Ernst was ten years old when he decided that his lessons were boring. His teachers told his parents that their son was "stupid".

WOODLICE HAVE BIGGER BRAINS

"So a teacher called him stupid – what's new?" I hear you say. Well, instead of giving young Ernst a hard time his mum and dad took him away from school and he grew up to be a scientific genius. It might be worth trying this story on your parents – but I doubt it will work.

Ernst's dad bred silkworm caterpillars to make silk and was also very keen on science. His mum loved art and poetry, and between them they taught young Ernst at home. The boy learnt his lessons in the morning and in the afternoon he helped with the silkworms.

At 15 Ernst went back to school where science became his favourite subject. He went on to teach science at university, but he was so poor that he decided to study the science of hearing for which he wouldn't need to buy expensive equipment. His own ears would do fine.

In 1887 Ernst was studying missiles that flew faster than sound waves. He found that at supersonic speeds (that means faster than sound) the wave of air pushed out in front of the missile changes direction.

This allowed the missile to travel smoothly at a supersonic speed.

By 1929 some scientists were dreaming of aeroplanes that could fly faster than sound. So they decided to honour Ernst's discovery by measuring speed in Mach numbers (Mach 1 was the speed of sound). But the scientists faced a dreadful problem. It seemed no human could ever travel that fast … and live.

THE CONE OF DEATH

Although, as Mach showed, a missile could fly at speeds faster than sound, there was a lot of bumpiness on the way. As a flying object nears the speed of sound the air forming the sound waves can't escape fast enough. The air piles up around the plane in a massive invisible cone. A cone of death. The shaking and buffeting of the air cone was enough to tear an ordinary plane to pieces.

By 1947 every pilot who had flown near the speed of sound had been killed. Pilots called it "the sound barrier".

But in a secret airfield in California, USA, one young man dreamed of breaking through the barrier in a specially strengthened plane that was designed for high-speed flight. Would tragedy strike again? If one of the project's engineers had kept a secret diary it might have read something like this:

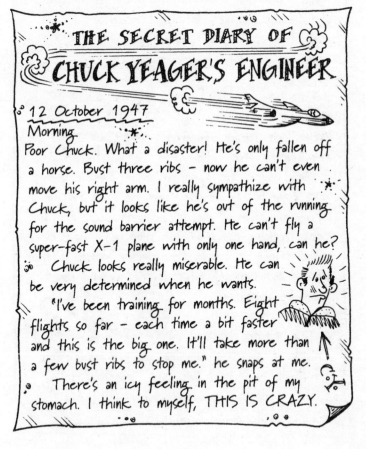

THE SECRET DIARY OF CHUCK YEAGER'S ENGINEER

12 October 1947

Morning

Poor Chuck. What a disaster! He's only fallen off a horse. Bust three ribs - now he can't even move his right arm. I really sympathize with Chuck, but it looks like he's out of the running for the sound barrier attempt. He can't fly a super-fast X-1 plane with only one hand, can he?

Chuck looks really miserable. He can be very determined when he wants.

"I've been training for months. Eight flights so far - each time a bit faster and this is the big one. It'll take more than a few bust ribs to stop me." he snaps at me.

There's an icy feeling in the pit of my stomach. I think to myself, THIS IS CRAZY.

But I know he'll try it anyway, so I figure I'd
better help.

Oooo ← me

Afternoon
The main trouble with Chuck's injuries is that
he can't reach far enough to close the X-1's
door with his left hand. I poke around in the
hanger and find a broomstick. I cut it to size
and Chuck manages to close the door
using the stick. Don't know how it'll
work at 20,000 feet though.

14 October
8.00 am
We're just taking off from
the bomber base. The X-1

LIKE
THIS →

is slung under the plane we're in. Chuck seems
very calm but I can see from his face he's in a
lot of pain. "I'm all right," he grimaces. "But I
keep thinking about all the pilots who have been
killed trying to break the barrier." Well, if that
doesn't put him off what will? I wish I could
think of something.

R.I.P.

? ? ?

A few minutes later. . .
This is it. Chuck's climbing down a ladder into
the X-1. Now that I've said "Goodbye" to
Chuck, I can't help wondering if I'll get a

chance to say "Hi, Chuck" again. My fingers are crossed.

Then I hear the click as the X-1's door locks smoothly. Three cheers for the broomstick handle! But if anything happens to Chuck . . . it'll be down to that piece of wood, and me. I helped him after all.

We can hear Chuck over the radio link with the X-1.

IT'S COLD!

"Brrr, it's cold," he complains.

Well, I'm not surprised, I think. *There's hundreds of gallons of liquid oxygen fuel on that plane. It has to be stored at −188°C (−307°F). That's cold enough to frost over the windshield from the inside. Lucky we hit on the shampoo idea. That was a neat trick! Squirt a layer of shampoo on the glass and it stops the frost from forming.*

10.50 am

"This is it," says the pilot of our plane nervously. He starts the countdown, "Five . . . four . . . three . . . two . . . one . . ."

My heart's in my mouth. Can Chuck really fly the X-1 with just one hand? Should I have stopped him?

WHOOSH

"DROP!"

Too late now he's on his way.

Chuck's got seconds to flick the ignition switch and start the X-1's engines. But if there's a spark near the fuel, the X-1 will be blown to bits. But the engine's firing perfectly. There she goes! Phew!

"I'm beginning to run," yells Chuck.

But we can't cheer yet.

He's hitting turbulence. Here comes the sound barrier – the next few moments are critical. Will the X-1 fall to pieces like the other planes? The seconds tick away... We hear only silence.

There's a sudden rumble. Is it thunder? No – it's the boom made as Chuck flies faster than sound. He's done it! The X-1's flying smoothly at Mach 1.05! HE'S BROKEN THE SOUND BARRIER! YES, YES, YES!!!

WHOOPEE!

BOOM

2.00pm

Glad to be back on solid ground. I'm shattered. Chuck has a huge grin all over his face. He looks on top of the world so I ask him how he's feeling.

"Not so bad!" he laughs.

Not so bad. Not so bad for a guy with three busted ribs!

BOOMING MARVELLOUS SONIC BOOMS

Chuck Yeager had proved people can travel smoothly and safely at speeds faster than sound. And today military jet planes regularly break the sound barrier.

If this happens near you you'll hear all about it. Remember the sound like thunder made by Chuck's plane as it smashed through the sound barrier? You'll hear something similar. It'll rattle your windows, shake your chimney pots and possibly give your hamster a nervous breakdown. And the cause of this deadly force? Er – air. All those trillions of air molecules squashed together in front of the plane and fanning out behind it. When they hit the ground you hear this extraordinary sound. It's called a sonic boom.

Dare you discover ... how to hear a sonic boom?

Here's your chance to check out your very own sonic boom – otherwise known as a peal of thunder. Lightning is a searing hot spark caused by a build up of electricity in a storm cloud. This heats the surrounding air and makes a giant vibration that whizzes faster than sound. This makes the sonic boom we call thunder. Are you brave enough to probe its secrets?

RAIN, RAIN, RAIN, RAIN! WE NEED SOMETHING TO BRIGHTEN THINGS UP . . .

ARGH! FIRE! WE NEED MORE RAIN!

HORRIBLE HEALTH WARNING!

During this experiment try to avoid...

a) getting struck by lightning

b) getting soaked to the skin

c) giving your family a nasty fright

In fact, you can do it perfectly well at home. Just make sure all nervous parents, small brothers/sisters and family pets are safely indoors.

You will need:
A thunderstorm
Yourself
A watch with a second hand

What you do:
Watch the thunder and lightning.

1 *What do you notice?*
a) Thunder always comes before lightning.
b) Lightning always comes before thunder.
c) Thunder and lightning always happen at the same time.

Count the seconds between the lightning and the thunder.

2 *What do you notice?*
a) There's always the same time gap between the two.
b) The harder it rains the longer the gap becomes.
c) The time gap seems to get shorter or longer each time.

But if you think thunder's loud, there are noises in the next chapter that make thunder sound like a gnat burping! Get out your ear plugs (make sure they're clean, first!) and prepare to be SHATTERED!

SHATTERING SOUNDS

What's the loudest sound you've ever heard? Your little brother/sister bawling? Your grandad snoring? Or maybe you've heard something REALLY NOISY. Like a pop concert or a high speed train in a hurry. Here's a chart to compare the loudness of sounds.

TYPE OF NOISE	DECIBELS	EFFECT ON YOU →
You accidentally drop a sweet wrapper during a science lesson. WHOOPS!	10dB	So quiet no one notices. Phew! (Pick it up later)
You whisper to your friend during the lesson.	20-30dB	Sssh! People can hear you.
You start chatting to your friend. NATTER CHATTER!	60dB	Your teacher can hear you now. This could be painful.
The whole class starts chatting.	75dB	Ooh-er! Take cover!

Scientists measure the amplitude (loudness) of sound in bels and decibels (1 decibel=1 dB=10 bels). They're named after British-American inventor Alexander Graham Bell (1847–1922) (see page 105). By the way, just to confuse you, every time you go up three dB the sound gets about twice as loud. Got that? So 4 dB is roughly twice as loud as 1 dB.

We interrupt this chapter to bring you a really loud noise warning. Yes, it's even louder than the plane. It's just about to happen on the next page. GET DOWN! ARGHHHHHHHHHHHHHH!!!!!!!

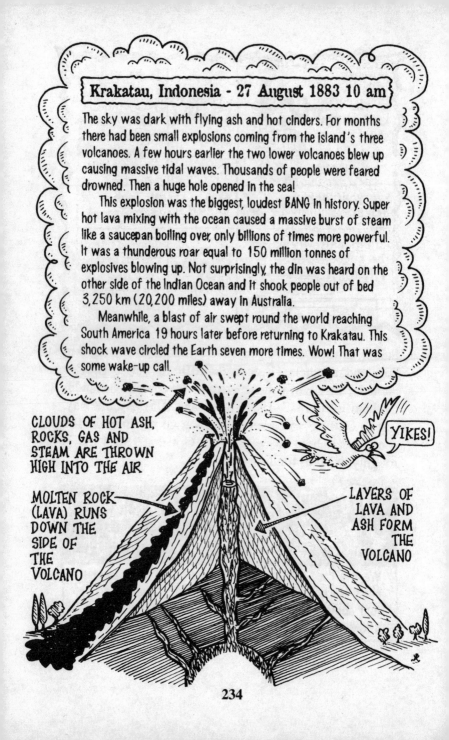

Krakatau, Indonesia - 27 August 1883 10 am

The sky was dark with flying ash and hot cinders. For months there had been small explosions coming from the island's three volcanoes. A few hours earlier the two lower volcanoes blew up causing massive tidal waves. Thousands of people were feared drowned. Then a huge hole opened in the sea!

This explosion was the biggest, loudest BANG in history. Super hot lava mixing with the ocean caused a massive burst of steam like a saucepan boiling over, only billions of times more powerful. It was a thunderous roar equal to 150 million tonnes of explosives blowing up. Not surprisingly, the din was heard on the other side of the Indian Ocean and it shook people out of bed 3,250 km (20,200 miles) away in Australia.

Meanwhile, a blast of air swept round the world reaching South America 19 hours later before returning to Krakatau. This shock wave circled the Earth seven more times. Wow! That was some wake-up call.

CLOUDS OF HOT ASH, ROCKS, GAS AND STEAM ARE THROWN HIGH INTO THE AIR

YIKES!

MOLTEN ROCK (LAVA) RUNS DOWN THE SIDE OF THE VOLCANO

LAYERS OF LAVA AND ASH FORM THE VOLCANO

234

TEACHER'S TEA-TIME TEASER

This terribly tasteless teatime teaser will set your teacher's teeth on edge. Tap quietly on the staff room door and when it groans open quietly ask:

I WAS JUST WONDERING WHY IT MAKES SUCH A HORRIBLE SCREECHING SOUND WHEN YOU SCRATCH YOUR FINGERNAILS DOWN THE BLACKBOARD?

GROAN!

Answer: Brr – it's enough to give you the shivers. In the mid-1980s scientists in Northwestern University, USA, played the sound to volunteers to find out why it was so bad. The fingernail rapidly touches tiny bumps on the board and sets off a mix of uneven high-frequency vibrations that sound dreadful. And maybe that's why it sets your teeth on edge.

NOISE NUISANCE

1 Are you being kept awake by noise? Maybe you've got noisy neighbours or a bawling baby brother or an anti-social parrot. Or maybe there's thundering traffic nearby? Cheer up, research shows you can sleep even when there's 40–60 dB of noise going on. If you're used to the noise, that is.

2 Nothing new about this. In ancient Rome, Julius Caesar passed a law to stop people driving noisy chariots about at night. They were keeping the citizens awake. But the chariot drivers didn't take any notice.

235

3 But louder noises are more of a headache – literally. Back in the 1930s, scientists found that factory workers worked harder when they wore ear-muffs to drown out noise. And people who worked in noisy places often felt bad-tempered after a hard day. (That's their excuse, anyway.)

4 Deafening noises can seriously damage your health. Scientists exposed to DREADFULLY LOUD sounds of 130 dB look a bit like this.

GIDDY →

130 dB

130 dB

SWOLLEN FINGER JOINTS

WOBBLING CHEST

NUMB HANDS AND FEET

5 In the 1970s, NASA scientists in the USA built a machine that made a racket registering 210 dB. (Fancy living next door to that?) The sound waves from this din were so powerful they could knock holes in solid objects.

6 In 1997 it was reported that US military bases in Britain were to be defended by powerful sound guns. Sound waves from these machines would make any intruder's intestines vibrate so much they'd need to find a toilet in a hurry. (Sounds dreadful!)

DON'T SUPPOSE YOU COULD LEND ME A CLEAN PAIR OF PANTS?

7 Scientists in France have developed an even deadlier weapon powered by an aircraft engine. It makes powerful infrasound waves – that's sounds too low for us to hear. But this sinister sound can make people feel sick and dizzy. The powerful sound vibrations shake the body's vital organs causing fatal damage. It can actually kill a person if they're less than 7 km away!

Hopefully such a horrific machine will never be fired – but ordinary sound has already been used as…

A SOUND WEAPON

In 1989 US forces invaded Panama, in Central America in a bid to arrest the suspected drugs dealer General Manuel Noriega. But the wily General, (nick-named "old pineapple face") had fled his luxury villa for the Vatican embassy. The Americans were stumped. They couldn't gatecrash the embassy to grab the General. It was against international law. So "old pineapple face" was safe. Or was he?

Someone had a seriously sound idea. Why not blast the General out with sound? Here's what their notes to the General might have looked like (if they'd sent any)...

Dear Pineapple face

You see those giant amplifiers outside your window? In 30 seconds we're going to start playing really loud music. We'll be blasting the embassy round the clock until you turn yourself in. Happy listening!

Love, the US forces
PS Any requests?

Dear Yankee loud-mouths

Ha, ha. You don't scare me. I love music – the louder the better...

Love, General Noriega XXXX
PS Got any opera?

Dear Pineapple face

OK, you've had your classical music. Now for some really heavy rock! Yeah – it's time for something seriously LOUD by sixties guitar legend Jimi Hendrix.

Hope you like it!

Love, the US forces
PS Got the message yet?
PPS Come out with your hands up!
And this one's for you, General.

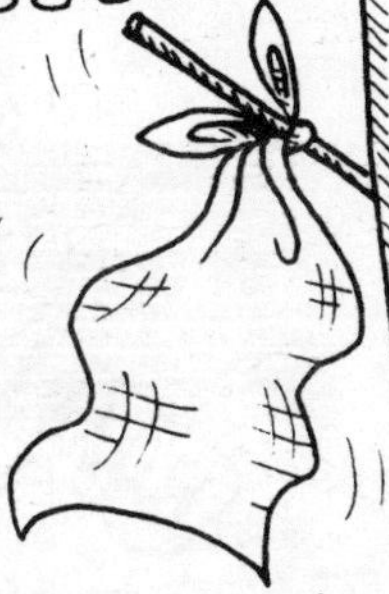

Dear No-good Yankees

Ow, my head hurts!
I can't stand it anymore.
I can't sleep, I can't think,
I can't eat. I'm going
crazy – I just can't take
it. OK, OK, you win. I surrender. Just
turn that dreadful noise down. Please!

Love, General Noriega
PS Got any headache pills?

239

Oh, so you like a bit of noise then? Really wild noise? Well, you'll lurve the next chapter. It's wild all right. Wild, woolly and hungry with huge bloodthirsty fangs. Are you wild enough to read on…? Howwwwwwwwl!

NOISY NATURE

Some people think that nature is quiet. Peaceful, tranquil, serene. But animals are never quiet. Their world is full of appalling growling, yowling, howling cries, and what's more they don't care if they keep you awake. Here's your chance to hear from some dreadfully loud wildlife.

The rowdy RATS

Famous for their squeaky songs. Some of them perform in ultrasound – that's notes too high-pitched for us to hear. They will be performing their traditional song of welcome to visiting rats,

SQUEAK! SQUEAK! SQUEAK! *

DON'T LIKE THE SOUND OF THIS MUCH

* "*Clear off you dirty rats or we'll kill you!*"
(The ultrasound version is a bit wasted on humans.)

QUACK! CUCKOO! TWITTER! CHIRRUP! CHIRP! OH DEAR!

The sensational SONG BIRDS

Hear them warble away with their amazing singing syrinxes (see-rinx-es) – that's the skin stretched over their windpipes. (It's the vibrations that make a whistling sound.)

(APOLOGY. The different types of birds are refusing to sing one song and insisting on singing their own tunes all at the same time. This may prove confusing.)

The high-flying HOWLER MONKEYS

Performing their hit single, *"Get lost you other monkeys – this is our patch!"* WARNING. These monkeys can be heard 15 km (9 miles) away. Members of the audience are respectfully advised to stick their fingers in their ears.

The charming cheeky CHIMPS

Will be performing their exciting new song, "Pant hoo, pant hoo, pant hoo." Roughly translated this means, *"Come over here, there's some scrumptious fruit on this tree."*

THE ORCHESTRA
(PERCUSSION SECTION)

The wild and wonderful WOODPECKERS

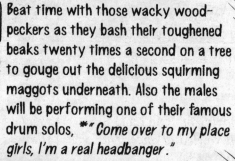

PECK! PECK! PECK! PECK!*

Beat time with those wacky woodpeckers as they bash their toughened beaks twenty times a second on a tree to gouge out the delicious squirming maggots underneath. Also the males will be performing one of their famous drum solos, *"Come over to my place girls, I'm a real headbanger."

The crazy clicking male CICADAS (chick-ard-ers)

They'll be playing the vibrating skin inside their abdomens, "TSH-ee-EEEE e-ou." Roughly translated this means, *"Here I am, come and get me, you lovely lady cicadas!"*

TSH-ee-EEEE-e-ou

(WARNING. These cicadas are very loud - more than 112 dB. Members of the audience are advised to take cover under their chairs.)

SPECIAL ANNOUNCEMENT

We apologize to readers who were looking forward to the first ever animal concert. It's been cancelled. Unfortunately some of the choir have been eating one another, and some members of the orchestra have escaped.

HOP IT!

Have you ever heard a grasshopper stridulate (strid-u-late)? If you answered, "I often stride when late," then read on. Stridulating is the sound grasshoppers make by rubbing their hairy little legs together. (No, your pet gerbil can't do this – I don't care if he has got hairy little legs.) Male grasshoppers stridulate to serenade fanciable female grasshoppers.

But even when grasshoppers make a racket it's really hard to tell exactly where they're hiding. Scientists have found that the frequency of the noise is about 4,000 Hz, and it so happens that humans aren't very good at judging the direction of these sounds. Higher-pitched sounds can be found using one ear, but for lower-

245

pitched sounds we use both ears. That's because longer sound waves bend around our heads. But with sounds in between we're a bit stuck. Well, we can't listen with one and a half ears can we?

Animals are a lot better at this hearing lark. They have to be. They've got to keep their ears open for smaller animals to scoff and for the heavy footfalls of hungry beasts out to scrunch them. Now 'ere's your chance to guess how good they are.

EAR, EAR

1 African elephants (the ones with big floppy ears) can hear better than Indian elephants (the ones with small floppy ears). TRUE/FALSE

NICE HAT!

2 Some moths have ears on their wings. TRUE/FALSE
3 Crickets have ears on their legs. TRUE/FALSE
4 Snakes have ears hidden under their scales. TRUE/FALSE
5 Frogs have ears … er, somewhere. TRUE/FALSE
6 An owl's face picks up sound like a large ear. TRUE/FALSE

7 Aardvarks have incredible hearing. They can hear termites scuttling about underground. TRUE/FALSE

8 Indian false vampire bats (I kid you not – that's what they're called) can hear tiptoeing mice. TRUE/FALSE

Answers: 1 FALSE. Larger ears don't help African elephants hear better but they do help keep them cool. Their big ears allow more blood to flow to just under the skin and so lose body heat into the outside air. **2** TRUE. Lacewing moths have ears on their wings. All insect ears are thin flaps of skin that vibrate in response to sound just like your ear drums. The vibes trigger nerves to send messages to the insect's tiny little brain. **3** TRUE And that's why you'll never see a cricket wearing spectacles. By the way, like grasshoppers, male crickets make sounds to attract females of the same species (type of insect) and so I guess they need their ears for a sound reason (groan!) **4** FALSE. Snakes don't have ears. They can't hear noises but they can sense the vibrations made by anything walking on the ground. Snakes pick up these signals through their jaw bones. **5** FALSE. Frogs don't have ears but they have ear drums on each side of their heads. Scientists have played different sounds to frogs. They found that frogs are best at picking up low frequency sounds – like croaks! **6** TRUE. An owl's face is shaped a bit like a satellite dish. It's brilliant at picking up sounds and bouncing them towards the owl's ear holes at the edge of the "dish". **7** TRUE. Then the aardvarks dig the termites up with their paws and lick them up with a long, sticky tongue. Tasteee! **8** TRUE. The bats swoop down and grab the mice. But the mice do have a chance – they can hear the bat's high-pitched calls.

247

CHATTING CETACEANS

Cetaceans (see-tay-shuns) is the posh word for whales and dolphins. Use it in a science lesson and you're bound to make a big splash.

Some of the most amazing animal calls are made by dolphins and whales. They moo like cows, trill like birds, and whistle like … er, whistles. They can even creak like a rusty old door hinge. All these sounds are made in rapid pulses of little more than a few milliseconds. But blue and fin whale calls can measure 188 dB. That's loud enough to damage your ears and be heard by other whales 850 km away.

We don't know what these sounds mean. They could be a way for the animals to keep in touch or chat to their friends. But some boring scientists have pointed out that cetaceans can make the sounds as soon as they're born. So they obviously don't learn a language like we do. They must learn something in a school of whales, though – ha ha!

TEACHER'S TEA-TIME TEASER

Tap gently on the staff room door and when it squeaks open smile sweetly and ask:

" 'SCUSE ME, I WAS JUST WONDERING HOW DOLPHINS AND WHALES SING UNDER WATER WITHOUT GETTING A MOUTHFUL OF OCEAN?"

SPLUTTER!

Answer: Your teacher can't sing with a mouthful of tea – I expect that's why she's spluttering instead. But whales and dolphins even manage to sing whilst chomping their breakfasts (you can't so don't try it). The sounds start in their throats and they force the air into bag-like structures linked to their nasal passages.

Dolphins and killer whales also make other, even stranger sounds. They make weird ultrasound clicks. In the 1950s American scientists found that dolphins could find food at the bottom of a murky pool on a dark night. Tests showed the animals were making the clicks and then picking up the echoes from an object to find food.

Amazing things, echoes. Unearthly, ghostly sounds – scary voices without bodies, and by some eerie coincidence the next chapter's all about them.

LET'S GO!

EERIE ECHOES

Here's a treat if you like the sound of your own voice. Stand about 30 metres from a wall. Shout really loudly. Listen. Can you hear your own voice echoing from the wall? Sounds kind of eerie, doesn't it?

EERIE ECHO FACTS

1 An echo is made by sound waves bouncing off a surface in the same way as light bounces off a mirror.

2 So where's the best place to hear echoes? Well, why not try an eerie old castle? There's one near Milan, Italy, where you can hear your voice echoing over forty times. The old walls trap the sound waves so they continue bouncing backwards and forwards.

3 The domes of St Paul's Cathedral, London, and the Capitol building in Washington, USA, both feature eerie whispering galleries. You can whisper something against the walls and someone across the dome can hear your whispers. The curve of the walls directs the echoes to a single point on the other side. So if you want to whisper a joke about your teacher make sure they are safely out of the building.

SIR'S A BIT LIKE ST PAUL'S ...AN ANCIENT STRUCTURE WITH A SMOOTH DOME ON TOP

I'LL SEE YOU ON THE COACH, MISS WATKINS!

4 Alpine horns, the incredibly long horns that people play in Switzerland, use echoes to boost their range by several kilometres. The eerie echoes rumble around the mountains, and they can be used to send simple messages.

5 Fog horn echoes also have an eerie message. The low-pitched notes of the fog horn carry a long distance and any echoes will bounce off cliffs and rocks, warning of deadly danger ahead.

6 There's nothing more eerie than the booming rumble of thunder. Much of this sound is made by echoes rebounding off clouds from the original peal of thunder.

7 But there's more to echoes than noise. Music also requires echoes to come eerily alive...

DESIGN YOUR OWN CONCERT HALL

Well CONGRATULATIONS, your school has just been awarded a special grant to build a new concert hall, and you've been asked to lend a hand with the design. Got any ideas? It's important to plan the inside carefully so people can hear music clearly. This is known as acoustics. Fortunately, we've got Jez Liznin to advise us.

1 The first thing we need is a big tank of water. You can make a ripple and watch it bounce from the walls of the tank.

2 Now let's look at the walls. Let's go for a curved wall around the back of the stage.

3 Avoid flat, smooth walls in your design. You'll get loads of echoes bouncing around in the wrong places – it'll be like being stuck in a tunnel.

4 Avoid comfy chairs and carpets and curtains. They'll soak up the sound and make the music sound rather dead. Hard chairs are better for the acoustics even if they do give you a sore bum.

5 Yes, that's right. You've got to build it. Didn't we tell you? Don't work too hard! Byeee!

DREADFUL EXPRESSIONS

Should you call the police?

Answer: No. Destructive interference is when two sets of sound waves cancel one another out. The second wave comes between the gaps in the first set of sound waves. As a result you can't hear either properly. You get this in badly designed concert halls.

But, of course, there's more to echoes than music. Sometimes echoes can mean life or death. If you're a bat, that is.

COULD YOU BE A SCIENTIST?

Scientists have been keen on bats for years. So is it true all scientists are seriously batty? In 1794, for example, Swiss scientist Charles Jurinne found that bats couldn't find their way around obstacles when they had their ears blocked.

But it wasn't until the 1930s that US scientist Donald R Griffin recorded a bat's ultrasound squeaks and proved they found their way around in the dark by listening to the echoes. Can you imagine flying dolphins?

One of many batty experiments carried out by batty scientists involved trying to confuse bats by playing noise. What do you think happened?

a) The bats stopped flying and slumped to the ground.

b) The bats flew more slowly and made more noise themselves.

c) The bats beat the scientists with their leathery wings.

Answer: b) It takes more than a bit of noise to bother a bat. But the bats were put off a bit because they did fly more carefully than usual.

Bet you never knew!
Different types of bat squeak on different frequencies and amplitudes. For example, the little brown bat has a call as loud as a smoke detector. (No, don't get any ideas – it's cruel to use bats as safety equipment.) But the whispering bat has a call that's only as loud as … believe it or not … a whisper. But whatever they call it, any bat could mean dreadful danger – if you happen to be a moth.

THE TIGER MOTH SURVIVAL MANUAL

by Squadron Leader Irma Tiger-Moth

> OK, AIR CREW, PAY ATTENTION TO THIS BRIEFING. IT COULD MEAN THE DIFFERENCE BETWEEN LIFE AND DEATH.

Here's your main enemy – a bat. Take a good look. Ugly looking blighter isn't he? Could be the last thing you see. So remember – Biting Bats Scoff Moths. They open their mouths wide and scrunch us with their sharp little fangs. What a terrible way to go! No wonder we moths are miffed.

a bat

MAKE SURE YOU LEARN THE FOLLOWING PROCEDURES BY HEART

1 Listen hard for bat squeaks. They mean there's a bat about, and it's flying your way! Luckily, you can hear the bats before they detect you so RUN FOR IT – er, I mean FLY FOR IT!

 SQUEAK

2 If the bat gets too close activate your vesicles. These are those tiny ridge plates on each side of your body, in case you didn't know. Squeeze 'em hard and the ridges make a loud pop noise. This'll confuse the bat. Ha, ha – serves 'em right.

3 While the bat's working out what's going on – you make your escape. It's best to drop to the ground. The cowardly bat will be too scared of crashing to follow you. Also, their echo sounders can't spot you on the ground. That's because they get so many echoes from the ground they can't make out which echoes are bouncing off you.

PHEW!

I GIVE UP!

Eventually, millions of years after bats and dolphins had the idea – humans decided to use echoes to find things. Or at least one brainy French scientist did.

Hall of fame: Paul Langevin (1872–1946)
Nationality: French

Young Paul was one of those kids who's always top of the class. He never came second in anything. Makes you sick, doesn't it? So I won't even tell you about how he taught himself Latin. Yuck! When Paul grew up he studied science at Cambridge University, England.

In 1912, a giant liner, the *Titanic*, sank after smashing into an iceberg, and over one thousand people drowned. After that catastrophe Langevin became interested in the idea of using sound waves to find a hidden object. He reckoned that sound waves could have been used to spot the iceberg. So in 1915, Langevin developed his idea into the invention later known as SONAR (which stands for SOund NAvigation and Ranging).

A machine called a transducer makes a kind of PING noise (too high for human ears to make out) and the sound waves from this bounce off underwater objects like shipwrecks, shoals of fish, whales, submarines and scuba diving elephants.

SOUND WAVES HIT OBJECT AND BOUNCE BACK

SONAR SENDS SOUND WAVES DOWNWARDS

The echoes are picked up by the transducer and turned into electrical impulses.

A receiver then measures the strength of the echoes and the time they took to reach the ship. The stronger the echo, the more solid the underwater object and the longer it takes to return, the more distant the object. Got all that? You can see the position of the object on a screen and find out how it's moving. Sound idea!

But sadly instead of helping to save lives, Langevin's invention helped to kill people. During the Second World War, SONAR was used to track down enemy submarines so that they could be destroyed with underwater bombs called depth charges.

Then in 1940, the Germans invaded France and Langevin found himself up to his ears in danger. His son-in-law opposed the take-over but he was executed. Then Langevin and his daughter were arrested. Surely, it was only a matter of time before the scientist faced the death penalty. Scientists around the world sent messages of support for Langevin and the Germans decided to lock him up in his own home. But he was still in danger and, helped by some brave friends, he escaped to Switzerland.

Today SONAR is still used to find underwater objects and in 1987 it faced its greatest test. Could SONAR locate the legendary monster in Loch Ness, Scotland? Mention the Loch Ness monster to most scientists and they sigh rather sadly and say, 'Oh, not that old chestnut!'

If there is a monster, say the scientists, how come there's no scientific proof like a dead monster's body? But just imagine there *was* a monster. And just imagine if this super-intelligent, super-sensitive creature could tell its own story? Here's what it might say…

"TROUBLED WATERS"

by Nessie 9-10 October 1987

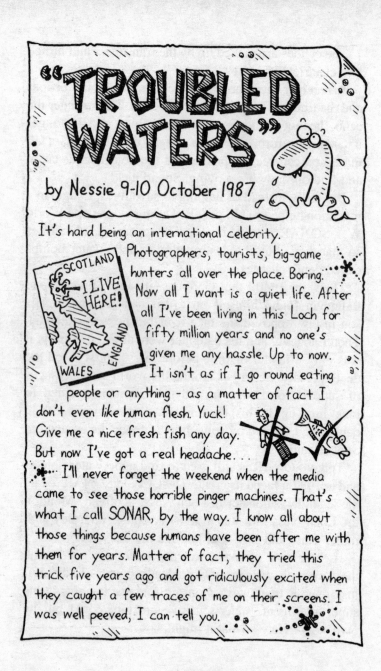

It's hard being an international celebrity. Photographers, tourists, big-game hunters all over the place. Boring. Now all I want is a quiet life. After all I've been living in this Loch for fifty million years and no one's given me any hassle. Up to now.

It isn't as if I go round eating people or anything - as a matter of fact I don't even like human flesh. Yuck! Give me a nice fresh fish any day. But now I've got a real headache...

I'll never forget the weekend when the media came to see those horrible pinger machines. That's what I call SONAR, by the way. I know all about those things because humans have been after me with them for years. Matter of fact, they tried this trick five years ago and got ridiculously excited when they caught a few traces of me on their screens. I was well peeved, I can tell you.

SCOTLAND
I LIVE HERE!
WALES   ENGLAND

260

Of course, I never dreamt they'd try again. I was having a quiet little swim - as you do. I mean, the Loch might be deep and dark and freezing cold and gloomy but it's home to me. Anyway, I poked my head up above water for a quick nose about and that's when I saw them. Hundreds of journalists, dozens of boats, helicopters, TV cameras - the works. You could have knocked me down with a dead haddock. Luckily, they were all listening to a big guy with a bushy beard. Otherwise I'd have been spotted.

Matter of fact, I know the big guy. Adrian Shine is his name. He's a scientist and he's been trying to spot me for years. (Ha, ha, you should be so lucky, Ade.) Anyway, he was telling the pilots of the boats to, "Form a line across the loch and keep on going at a steady speed." Blimey - he even had flags on either bank to keep the boats in line - and those blinkin' pingers. Every boat had one. Noise? Huh, all that pinging all day long - I got a MONSTER headache!

flags

line of boats with SONAR

I know they spotted me a couple of times. I was hiding about 150 metres down. *That should be enough,* I thought. But I should have realized, this stupid SONAR noise goes down hundreds of metres. Anyway, I heard a ping really close and up above they were all shouting:

"It's a monster - he's down there!"

He? Blooming cheek - I'm a SHE!

So I beat a hasty retreat. But that night I surfaced and heard people talking - it was a press conference. A couple of American SONAR experts were sounding very puzzled about the signals. One said they don't look as if they've been made by fish.

Fish? Grrr, I'm not a FISH - but what did he know?

Anyway, they managed to ping me next day too, but then I made myself really scarce. Didn't want to get myself caught on SONAR again, did I?

I mean, just imagine if they got some real proof that I existed. The autograph hunters, TV wildlife documentaries, royal visits. It's not going to happen. I'm going to skulk in my cosy underwater cave until they've gone home. Yeah, push off humans, can't you see I want to be alone?

LOCH NESS · THE DREADFUL TRUTH

The SONAR sweep of Loch Ness covered two-thirds of the vast loch. It had been thorough and well-planned. But the dreadful truth was that it failed to prove Nessie existed. All the scientists had to show for their hard work was a few marks on a sonar chart. The charts were computer print-outs from a sonar screen and the marks showed moving solid objects. Could these be traces of an unknown creature? A large creature bigger than any known type of fish. The file on the Loch Ness monster remains open.

So what would you do if you managed to spot a huge monster unknown to science. Would you…
a) shout for joy
b) say hello
c) scream for your Mummy?

Chances are you'd want to make some kind of sound. Wanna know how? Better clear your throat and read the next chapter.

DREADFUL BODY SOUNDS

It's great being you, isn't it? You can make so many smashing noises. Some are musical, some aren't and some are just plain rude. After you make a rude noise have you noticed that that's when your friends make noises, too? Those strange shuddering, tinkling, squeaking, braying sounds we call "laughter".

DREADFUL BURPS, FARTS AND RASPBERRIES
Here's how to make some entertaining body noises, but **don't** make them...
a) In a science lesson

b) In school assemblies or dinner times
c) When the posh relatives come for lunch

Otherwise you'll never hear the end of it.

Farting

Made by vibrating skin around your bottom as air rushes out. You can make similar noises by putting your mouth over your arm and blowing hard.

FAAAART!

Snoring

SNORE!

UVULA

Made by the uvula (that's the dangling bit at the back of your throat). If a person sleeps on their back with their mouth open, their deep breathing makes the uvula flutter. You can make a disgusting snoring sound by lying in this position and breathing in.

Bet you never knew!

So you think your dad/uncle/grandad/pet pot-bellied pig snores like a pneumatic drill? Huh – that's nothing! In 1993, Kare Walkert of Sweden was recorded snoring at 93 dB. That's louder than a really noisy disco. By the way, the best thing to do with someone who snores isn't to hit them over the head. No, all you do is gently close their mouths and turn them on their sides. Ahh, peace, perfect peace!

ZZZZZZZz

Burping

The air comes up not from your lungs but from your stomach. The vibrations from the gullet (the food passage from your mouth to your stomach) gives the burp its unique and rather endearing tone. To burp, try pushing in your tummy and opening your mouth wide. It helps if you've just scoffed your lunch in five seconds then slurped a fizzy drink.

Whistles and humming

These aren't exactly rude, but I suppose it depends where you do them. For example, it wouldn't be a good idea to whistle the tune to "The Sound of Music" when you were at church.

Humming is caused partly by a particular set of vibrations in the skin inside the nostrils. Try pinching your nose as you hum and you'll hear how important this is.

Whistles are caused by air whistling though the round hole made by your lips forming little whirlwinds in your mouth that make its inside vibrate.

Talking about vibrating insides, there's lots of fascinating sounds going on inside your body…

SOUNDS UNHEALTHY

One day in 1751, Austrian doctor Leopold Auenbrugg (1727–1809) happened to notice a wine merchant tapping a barrel. The merchant explained that the sound told him how full the barrel was. *Hmm*, thought the doctor, *I wonder if you could do this for the human body?*

After a lot of thought Leopold wrote a book. He'd figured out a new way to discover if the body was unhealthy. Here's your chance to try it, too.

Dare you discover … how to hear your own chest?

You will need:
Two tupperware boxes with lids (these represent your chest)
Your hands

What you do:
1 Half fill one box with water.
2 Place the middle finger of your left hand so it's lying flat on the lid of the empty box.

3 Tap the middle portion of this finger with the middle finger of your right hand. The tap should be a smart downwards flick of the wrist.

4 Try to remember the sound.

5 Now repeat steps 1–3 on the lid of the box half full of water.

What do you notice?

a) The two sounds are exactly the same.

b) The empty box makes a dull empty sound and the box with water makes a higher sound.

c) The empty box sounds more hollow, the box with water sounds duller.

Answer: c) Doctors can still use this method to check out what's going on inside your chest. If the chest sounds hollow like a drum it means there is air in the space around the lungs (there should be fluid there).

DREADFUL EXPRESSIONS

A doctor tells you…

I'LL HAVE TO DO SOME AUSCULATION

Should you scream and ask for a painkiller?

268

THE STUNNING STETHOSCOPE

For hundreds of years doctors had a simple way to listen to their patients' breathing and heartbeat.

But one day shy French doctor René Laënnec (1781–1826) found himself in an embarrassing situation.

In desperation Laënnec remembered seeing two boys playing with a hollow log. One boy tapped the log and the other listened to the sound at the other end.

So Laënnec figured that a tube might be a good way to hear sounds louder. He rolled up a newspaper.

Success! Laënnec heard the young lady's heartbeat loud and clear. He wrote a book about his new technique and became rich and famous.

Sadly, though, Laënnec fell ill. And the man who had done so much to help doctors treat chest diseases eventually died … of a chest disease.

Bet you never knew!
By listening through a stethoscope you can find out if a person has a whole range of dreadful diseases. For example, when someone with the lung disease bronchitis (bron-ki-tis), breathes they make a kind of bubbling, crackling noise. Some heartless doctors describe this dreadful sound as "bubble and squeak".

Sounds dreadful fact file

NAME: Your voice

THE BASIC FACTS: The sound waves of a voice are affected by the shape of its owner's skull and mouth, etc. So every voice is different.

THE DREADFUL DETAILS: People who have had their vocal chords removed can still talk. But their voices come out as a whisper.

Here's where your voice comes from...

SOUND ALTERED BY POSITION OF TONGUE, LIPS AND JAWS

Do you like talking? Sorry, silly question. I mean do ducks like water, do elephants like buns? Here's your chance to find out how you do this amazing thing – a chin-wag.

Dare you discover 1 ... how you talk?
You will need:
A voice (preferably your own)
A pair of hands (preferably your own)

What you do:
1 Put your thumb and second finger lightly on your throat so they are touching but not pressing on it.
2 Now start humming.

What do you notice?
a) My throat seems to swell up when I hum.
b) I can feel a tingling in my fingers.
c) I can't hum when I'm touching my throat.

Dare you discover 2 ... how your voice changes?
You will need:
A balloon
One pair of hands (you could use the same pair as in experiment one)

What you do:
1 Blow up the balloon.
2 Let some of the air out. It makes a brilliant farting sound. (No, not during assembly).
3 Now stretch the neck of the balloon and try again.

What do you notice?

a) No sound comes out.

b) The sound gets higher.

c) The sound gets louder.

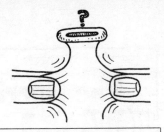

LEARN HOW TO TALK

OK, so you probably know how to do this anyway.

1 Try saying the letters A, E, I, O, U. Notice anything? The sounds are all made by complex air vibrations in your mouth.

2 Now say S, B, P. Notice what happens to your lips and tongue. Can you feel them moving? Can you say these letters without moving your tongue? Thought not.

3 Say N and M. Notice how part of the sound seems to come out of your nose. Try pinching your nose and notice what happens to the sound.

Keep going. With more practice you might do as well as these people…

273

The Horrible Science
Vocal Awards

RUNNER-UP: In 1990, Steve Woodmore of Orpington, England, spoke 595 words in 56.01 seconds. That's roughly all the words from here to page 278. Could you do this?

SECOND PRIZE: In 1988 Analisa Wragg of Belfast, Northern Ireland shouted at 121.7 dB – that's louder than a whole noisy factory. Bet she was cross about something.

CHAMPION: In 1983 Briton Roy Lomas whistled at 122.5 dB. That's louder than a small aircraft engine.

SOMETHING TO SHOUT ABOUT

Have you ever really shouted at someone really loud? I mean at the top of your voice – just as loud as you can. Of course you have. Maybe at the same time you spread your hands on either side of your mouth. Have you noticed how this makes your voice sound louder? A megaphone is only a cone with a hole in one end, but what a difference it makes. Here's how it works.

SOUND NORMALLY SPREADS OUT FROM YOUR MOUTH IN ALL DIRECTIONS

MEGAPHONE CHANNELS SOUND IN ONE DIRECTION SO IT SOUNDS LOUDER

MEGA-MOUTH MORLAND

The megaphone was the brainchild of wacky British inventor Samuel Morland (1625–1695). Sam had an amazing life – it was certainly something to sound off about. As a young man Morland worked for the government. It was a time when Britain was ruled by Oliver Cromwell and King Charles II was in lonely exile in France.

One night Morland overheard his boss and Oliver Cromwell hatching a plot to kill the king. Morland was scared and pretended to be asleep at his desk. Cromwell saw Morland and decided to kill him before he gave away the plot.

But Sam's boss persuaded Cromwell that the young man had been asleep. In 1660 Charles returned to power and Sam convinced the King he'd been on his side all along.

Sam became interested in science and built a powerful pump. He showed it off by squirting water and red wine over the top of Windsor Castle.

And he also invented the megaphone. One day the inventor got in a boat and shouted to the king from a distance of 0.8 km. History doesn't record what he said – it might have been something like this...

For hundreds of years the megaphone was the only way to make the human voice carry over large distances. And then someone made a re-sound-ing discovery.

Hall of fame: Alexander Graham Bell
(1847–1922) Nationality: British-American

Young Alexander Graham was bound to be fascinated by sound – it ran in the family. His dad was a Scottish professor who taught people with hearing difficulties to speak. This was handy because Alexander's mum also had hearing difficulties.

The young boy had a mind of his own. Aged only 11 he changed his name to Alexander Graham Bell in honour of a family friend. Unfortunately, having a mind of your own wasn't a good idea if you wanted to get on at school. Alexander hated the strict boring lessons. (Does this ring a bell with you?)

Alexander left school without any qualifications and thought about running away to sea. But then he had second thoughts and chose a life involving REAL hardship and deprivation. That's right – he became a teacher. This was quite surprising when you consider he was only 16 at the time – that's younger than some of his pupils. (But he looked older.)

In 1870 Alexander moved with his family to America and got a job teaching deaf children how to speak. Unlike some teachers Alexander was always kind and gentle and he NEVER lost his temper – sounds amazing!

But at nights he worked secretly on another interest. He began to dream of a new machine. A machine that could carry the human voice for hundreds of kilometres. A machine that would change the world for ever.

COULD YOU BE A SCIENTIST?

As a teenager, Alexander Graham Bell had a sound interest in science. Here are two of his favourite experiments. Can you predict the results?

1 Alexander and his brother built a talking machine. It was made of wood, cotton, rubber, a tin tube for the throat and a real human skull.

Alexander's brother blew air up the model's throat to supply puff to get the voice going. Alexander moved the

278

model lips and tongue to make the noises that we call speech. But would the machine work? What do you think?

a) The model never said a word – just a quiet hissing sound.

b) The model said, "Hi, dad!" in a clear voice. Alexander's dad saw the talking skull and fainted.

c) The model spoke in a Donald Duck-style voice.

2 Alexander decided to help his pet dog talk by moving its jaw and throat. How did he get on?

a) Terrible. The dog refused to say a word.

b) Smashing. Alexander was the first human to have an intelligent conversation with a dog.

c) The dog learnt how to ask, "How are you, grandmama?"

THAT RINGS A BELL

It's actually true that five hundred and ninety-nine people said they invented the telephone before Bell. Five hundred and ninety-eight of them were liars keen to cash in on the phone's success. But one of them, American born Elisha Gray, just happened to be telling the truth.

Elisha Gray was a professional inventor with his own firm part-owned by the Western Union Telegraph Company. He'd been thinking of ways to send sounds along electrical wires and had already made a few successful experiments.

One day in 1875, Gray saw two boys playing with a toy. It was two tin cans linked by a string. One boy would speak into a tin can and the string carried the sound waves to the other can which the other boy held to his ear. A light bulb flashed in the inventor's brain. He came up with an idea for transmitting not just sounds but actual voices along a wire. It was identical to Bell's design even though the two inventors had never met.

Gray managed to sketch out his idea on 11 February – that's a month before Bell put his thoughts on paper. So Gray was now on track to win fame and fortune. But meanwhile Bell and his assistant Thomas Watson were working flat out to build their machine. Their telephone was the result of two years' hard work. Its improvements were based on trial and error. It was made up of...

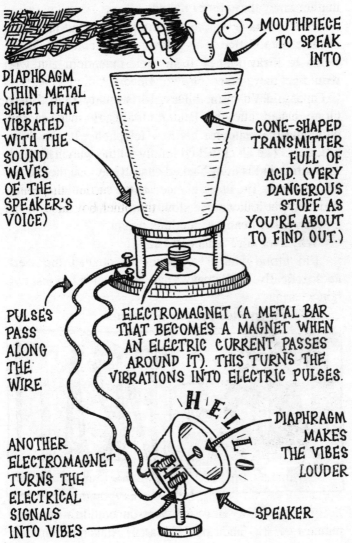

MOUTHPIECE TO SPEAK INTO

DIAPHRAGM (THIN METAL SHEET THAT VIBRATED WITH THE SOUND WAVES OF THE SPEAKER'S VOICE)

CONE-SHAPED TRANSMITTER FULL OF ACID. (VERY DANGEROUS STUFF AS YOU'RE ABOUT TO FIND OUT.)

PULSES PASS ALONG THE WIRE

ELECTROMAGNET (A METAL BAR THAT BECOMES A MAGNET WHEN AN ELECTRIC CURRENT PASSES AROUND IT). THIS TURNS THE VIBRATIONS INTO ELECTRIC PULSES.

HELLO

DIAPHRAGM MAKES THE VIBES LOUDER

ANOTHER ELECTROMAGNET TURNS THE ELECTRICAL SIGNALS INTO VIBES

SPEAKER

The race was on to grab the glory and win the huge cash prizes that would follow from the new technology. But neither inventor knew about the other, remember. So neither knew they were in a race.

The next stage was to file the plans of the invention at the Patent Office. This allows the inventor exclusive rights to make money from their invention. But who would get there first – Gray or Bell?

On a cold Valentine's Day, 14 February 1876, Elisha Gray rushed into the Patent Office. He was eagerly clutching the plans for his new telephone. It was 2 pm precisely. The clock ticked loudly on the wall. The clerk sat writing in his high-backed chair. Gray coughed to get his attention. The clerk glanced at the patent application and then put it down. He slowly shook his head.

"Sorry, sir, I can't accept this patent."

"Why ever not?" snapped Gray.

"I'm afraid you're too late," announced the clerk apologetically. Bell's patent had been handed in just two hours earlier.

"DRAT!" shouted the foiled inventor.

But meanwhile Bell and Watson couldn't get their phone to work. Then on 10 March, Alexander Graham

Bell slopped some acid from the phone speakers on his clothes and made the world's first telephone call by accident.

"Mr Watson, come here I want you!" he yelled, perhaps adding under his breath, "and this acid's eating my trousers."

Thomas Watson ran to the aid of his boss whose faint and crackling voice he heard through the strange machine.

This was the call that launched a million chat lines. A defining moment in modern history. But when Bell rang Watson he hadn't rehearsed the words that would change the world, and he hadn't planned to dissolve his pants either.

(Some boring historians point out that Watson didn't get round to telling this story until 50 years later. So was it true? Perhaps. Maybe Watson kept it quiet until then to avoid making his good friend Bell look like a dumb-Bell.)

So Watson got a bell from A Bell and Elisha Gray was beaten to the bell. In 1877, Gray and the Western Union Telegraph Company took legal action against Bell and his backers claiming that Gray had got to the telephone first. Who would win? Would Bell get his just desserts or would Gray's story ring true with the judge?

What do you think?
a) The judge agreed with Gray. Bell's claim was phone-y and he had to give all his profits to Gray's company, leaving Bell penniless.
b) Gray and Bell agreed to split the money fifty-fifty. It was a fair dial – er, sorry deal.
c) Gray lost and had to call it a day. He didn't get a bean.

DREADFULLY SUCCESSFUL

The telephone was an instant smash-hit. By 1887 there were 150,000 telephones in the USA alone. For its inventors it was a chance to ring in the profits. But for Alexander Graham Bell personally it was a nightmare come to life. He once said:

Financial dealings are distasteful to me and not at all in my line.

The point was, Bell was happier just being a scientist. So at the ripe old age of 33 he retired to devote the rest of his life to scientific research. And he came up with plenty more inventions including:

• A probe to find bullets stuck in the body.
• An idea for making water from fog.
• A super-fast hydrofoil boat.

Bell loved machines and gadgets but one gadget in particular got on his nerves: he never allowed a phone near his lab. It was, he said, a distraction from his work.

Bet you never knew!
In the early days of telephones there were attempts to use them to broadcast music. In 1889, a company in Paris used phone lines to broadcast concerts to loudspeakers in hotels. The audience had to put money in the machines to get to the end of the piece. Sounds dreadful.

But it's not as bad as some of the dreadful musical moments you'll find in the next chapter. Can you stand crazy concerts, mad musicians and hideous clashing discords? If not, stuff a big wad of cotton wool in your ears and read on anyway.

DREADFUL MUSICAL MAYHEM

It's official! 99.9 per cent of us reckon music is smashing. Yes, great music can make our hearts jump for joy. It makes the world dance and sing, and laugh or even cry with its beauty. And bad music? Well, that's just a pain between the ears.

COULD YOU BE A SCIENTIST?

A scientist at the University of California, USA, used a computer to show patterns of nerves firing in the brain. His colleague suggested making the computer play the pattern in the form of sounds. And amazingly, these sounded just like classical music. So the scientists wondered whether listening to classical music could actually make the nerves work more effectively. Could the brain work better?

BRAIN WORKING TOO SLOWLY? TRY
Classical Music
Listen and become an amazing swotty brainbox!!
← BEFORE   AFTER →

The scientists decided to test the idea by giving three groups of students some tricky questions.

Group 1 had ten minutes of silence before they started.

Group 2 listened to a voice tape designed to make them more relaxed.

Group 3 listened to ten minutes of classical music by Mozart.

Which group did best in the tests?

a) Group 1. Any sound puts the brain off. That's why people need peace and quiet to work.

b) Group 2. The brain is best stimulated by the sound of a human voice.

c) Group 3. The theory was correct!

Answer: c) These students scored 8-9 points above the others. Could this help you in a science test? In 1997 scientists in London found that children aged nine to 11 learn more easily when there's soothing music in the background. So why don't teachers use it to liven up science lessons?

Research shows that listening to music can boost mental performance owing to a similarity between sound waves and nerve signal patterns.

A DISGUSTING DIN?

Despite the possible brain-boosting powers of music, every musician has had to put up with lots of unkind people who hated their work. It just goes to show that good music like good food is really a matter of taste.

Here's just one example – German composer Richard Wagner (1813–1883). Wagner composed grand and often incredibly loud music for huge orchestras. He had many fans but some people thought Wagner's music was worse than toothache. "Wagner has beautiful moments but awful quarter hours," commented GA Rossini (1792–1868). Other comments on the subject of Wagner's music were:

"I love Wagner, but the music I prefer is that of a cat . . . outside a window and trying to stick to the panes of glass with its claws."

Charles Baudelaire (1821–1867)

Mark Twain (1835–1910) thought Wagner's music sounded dreadful:

". . .at times the pain was so exquisite I could hardly keep the tears back. At those times, as the howlings and wailings and shriekings of the singers and the ragings and roarings and explosions of the vast orchestra rose higher and higher . . . I could have cried."

I expect your music teacher feels the same during school orchestra and school choir practice. And talking about great musicians, are you still itching to become a pop star? Brilliant, 'cos it's time to re-join Jez and Wanda in the sound studio to tackle the next stage of your training – learning to sing. (Admittedly some pop stars don't bother with this bit, but it can help!)

COULD YOU BE A POP STAR? STEP 2: SINGING

Wanda's just explaining the science of singing:

It's actually harder than you might think to become an expert singer, but these few tips should help:

1 First choose a song to practise. It helps if you know the tune and at least some of the words.

2 Stand with your head back and your shoulders back. Breathe in deeply to the pit of your tummy. Easy, innit?
3 Now it gets a bit trickier. Start singing. Carry on with the deep breathing as you sing. Try to open your mouth more widely than you usually do when you speak.
4 You'll find it's easier to produce higher and clearer notes if you smile whilst you sing. Try it and see.

5 OK, that's enough singing. I SAID THAT'S ENOUGH!
Now here's the hard bit: singing in tune (some people
never get this far). Try singing the same note as a key on
the piano or a note on a recorder. Can you get it right? On
a piano the keys are arranged in order of pitch. You may
know them as…

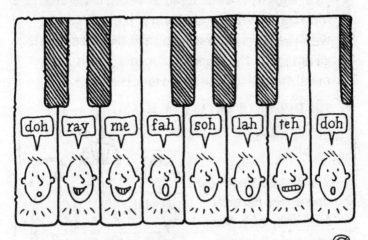

Bet you never knew!
Isn't it amazing you can still hear a singer even when
an orchestra is blasting out sound? Surely the roar of
all the different instruments ought to drown out the
singer's voice? But it doesn't and the reason why is
that a trained singer can produce sound at 2,500 Hz
– that's five times higher than most of the sound made
by the orchestra. So you hear the singer clearly.

But the most amazing musical secret is in the vibes.
Yep, we're talking about resonance again … but *beware*
this info could really SHAKE you up.

Sounds dreadful fact file

NAME: Resonance

THE BASIC FACTS: Everything has a natural frequency. That's the speed at which it vibrates most easily. When sound waves hit an object with the same natural frequency the object starts vibrating. So the sound gets louder. This is how most musical instruments work (see page 122).

THE DREADFUL DETAILS: 1 If you sing at a certain pitch the resonance starts your eyeballs vibrating.

2 A trained singer can sing at the natural frequency of a glass and make it vibrate. Some singers can even smash the glass if they sing loudly enough.

WHAT DO YOU THINK?

SMASHING!

LAAH!

Dare you discover ... how to make sounds resonate?

You will need:
A sea shell shaped like this...

What you do:
Put it to your ear and listen.
What is causing those eerie sound effects?

a) The ghostly echoes of the sea.

b) It's the sounds around you resonating in the shell.

c) These are faint sounds stored by chemical structures in the shell and released by the heat of your body.

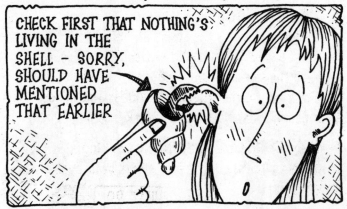

CHECK FIRST THAT NOTHING'S LIVING IN THE SHELL – SORRY, SHOULD HAVE MENTIONED THAT EARLIER

COULD YOU BE A POP STAR? STEP 3: MUSICAL INSTRUMENTS

To be a real star it might help to do more than just sing. In fact, why not learn a few instruments so you can really impress your fans? In the sound studio Jez and Wanda are comparing notes on musical instruments.

STRINGS AND THINGS

A stringed instrument is made up of strings stretched tight over an empty case.

ACOUSTIC GUITAR

STRINGS

EMPTY CASE

VIOLIN

DOUBLE BASS

TRADITIONAL VIOLIN STRINGS WERE MADE FROM DRIED CAT'S GUTS

YIKES!

295

DREADFUL EXPRESSIONS

A scientist says…

I'VE ALWAYS WANTED A CHORDOPHONE (KOR-DO-FONE) LIKE THIS

Can you really buy chord phones that look like violins?

Answer: No. A chordophone is the posh term for a stringed instrument like the violin. It means " stringed sound" in Greek. By the way, woodwind instruments are aerophones (air-ro-fones) (not aeroplanes – dimwit), brass instruments and drums are membranophones (mem-brain-o-fones) and percussion instruments are idiophones (i-deo-fones). No, that doesn't mean that they're played by idiots – even if these instruments seem easier to play.

A QUICK MUSICAL INTERLUDE

You've probably seen someone "tickling the ivories" of a piano before. You might even have had a go yourself. But did you know that the piano is also a type of stringed instrument? Here's how it works…

1 Press a key on the piano and you set in motion a series of levers.
2 The levers lift a hammer that strikes a tightly stretched wire to sound the note.

But things can go wrong. For example, damp air can make the felt between the piano keys take in moisture and swell up. The keys stick together and the pianist plays two notes instead of one. Then you get dreadful scenes of mayhem. This is what really happened at the Erawan Hotel in Bangkok, Thailand…

You'll be pleased to know that Mr Kropp was stopped from totally wrecking the piano by the Hotel Manager, two security guards and a passing police officer. If you're having piano lessons I hope this doesn't give you any ideas.

WARBLING WIND INSTRUMENTS

To make a really mellow sound you'll probably need more than just stringed instruments. How about adding a few woodwind instruments to your line up? A funky saxophone, a cool clarinet or a soulful flute.

Note: Woodwind instruments were once made from wood – that's how they get their name. Now they're often made from metal or other materials.

Wanda has volunteered to show us how to play a few wind instruments. Ever tried to play a milk bottle? That's a bit like blowing into a flute. You need to blow across the top:

BLOWING OVER THE HOLE MAKES THE AIR IN THE FLUTE VIBRATE

SPLUTTER!

DRIBBLE!

Well, in theory the air inside the flute vibrates to make the sound. In a saxophone or clarinet a reed in the mouthpiece vibrates when you blow to get the same effect.

WHEEZE!

COVERING THE HOLES STOPS THE AIR ESCAPING AND ALTERS THE NOTE

VIBRATING REED MAKES AIR INSIDE THE SAXOPHONE VIBRATE

PUFF!

A deeper sound comes out. Larger things make a lower sound when they vibrate, remember.

BRILLIANT BRASS

A fanfare of trumpets would really add some oomph to your hit. Brilliant brass instruments include…

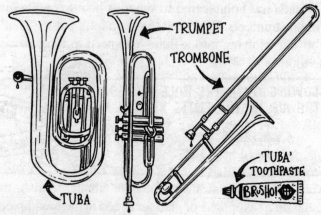

TRUMPET

TROMBONE

TUBA' TOOTHPASTE

BR-SHO!

TUBA

Like woodwind instruments you get the sound from air vibrating inside the instrument. But the vibes come from the special way you move your lips. By blowing a raspberry – here's Wanda's attempt.

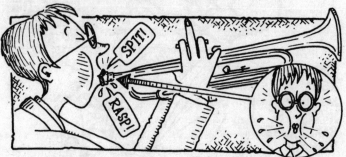

SPIT!

RASP!

You make higher sounds by pressing your lips tighter during the raspberry. Lengthening the pipe makes a deeper sound. You do this by pushing out the sliding part of the trombone or pressing the valve buttons on the trumpet and tuba.

TEACHER'S TEA-TIME TEASER

Are you feeling brave? Now's your chance to sound your teacher out on a vital scientific question. Hammer boldly on the staff room door and when it grinds open smile sweetly and say:

I WAS JUST WONDERING WHY YOUR KETTLE HISSES WHEN IT'S JUST ABOUT TO BOIL AND STOPS WHEN THE WATER IS BOILING?

GROAN!

Answer: Hopefully, your teacher will not be boiling with anger at this interruption. The answer to your question is like a wind instrument, the sound is caused by vibrating air. Bubbles rise in the water as it heats up and collapse as they get to the surface. The air vibrates in the kettle and makes the sounds you hear. When the water has boiled the bubbles don't collapse and the sound stops.

PECULIAR PERCUSSION

Percussion instruments include anything that you can bash together to make sounds. Like...

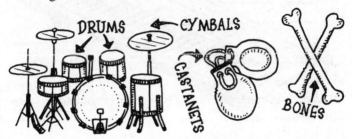

DRUMS ← CYMBALS

CASTANETS

BONES

301

Now how about a serious drumbeat? It'll give a great rhythm to your track. It's easy to make a sound on the drums – you just hit them with drumsticks. (No, not chicken drumsticks.)

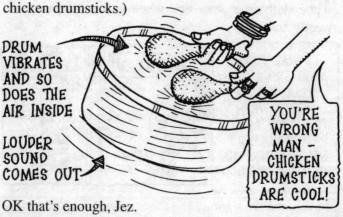

DRUM VIBRATES AND SO DOES THE AIR INSIDE

LOUDER SOUND COMES OUT

YOU'RE WRONG MAN – CHICKEN DRUMSTICKS ARE COOL!

OK that's enough, Jez.

Bet you never knew!
Can't decide which instrument to play? Just imagine an awesome machine that can make the sound of any instrument in the world. Impossible? No it's really true – it's called a synthesizer.

This is what it looks like:

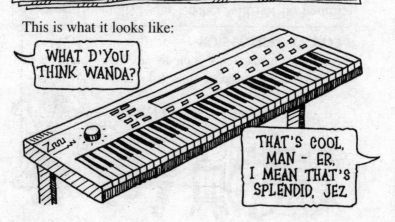

WHAT D'YOU THINK WANDA?

THAT'S COOL, MAN – ER, I MEAN THAT'S SPLENDID, JEZ

Here's how to use it:

1 It's amazing, you just set the controls for the type of instrument you want to play.

2 The synthesizer makes electronic signals that get stronger and weaker just like the sound waves of the instrument you want to copy.

3 The signals go to an amplifier and are turned into sounds. The sounds are strangely similar to your chosen instrument.

4 The synthesizer has keys so you can play it like a piano. But it can sound very different.

SUPER SAMPLERS AND MIXING

Playing music was fun but here's the tricky bit. You've got to record the various instruments and mix the tracks together. Jez can do this with the help of a fantastic brain-boggling machine. Or more accurately *two* fantastic mind-boggling machines in one.

CONTROLS FOR SAMPLING SOUNDS AND MIXING THEM TOGETHER

I CAN SAMPLE MIKE'S MIAOW THEN PLAY A TUNE IN 'CAT' ON THE KEYBOARD

The mixer allows Jez to record, or dub, the sound of your voice over the sound of the instruments.

The sampler part of the machine can take ANY sound – an annoying yowling cat for example – and play it back at a different speed. The sampler makes a sound more echoey; it can even play sound backwards. With a sampler your singing will sound even more brilliant.

So how do you feel? Are you bursting to make a big noise? Or in need of a nice cup of tea and a couple of headache pills? Jez and Wanda will be back with some even more serious sound machines later. But for now, keep your earplugs firmly in place. 'Cos the next chapter is LOUD and it really does sound *dreadful*.

DREADFUL SOUND EFFECTS

Here's what you've been waiting for – the chance to blow your own trumpet … and everything else too. You don't need posh and expensive instruments to make your own music. The good news is you can make interesting and rather horrible sound effects using everyday objects.

ODD ORCHESTRA QUIZ

Musicians have used some really strange things and some really dreadful things to make "musical" instruments. Which of these "instruments" has never been played in a public performance? TRUE/FALSE

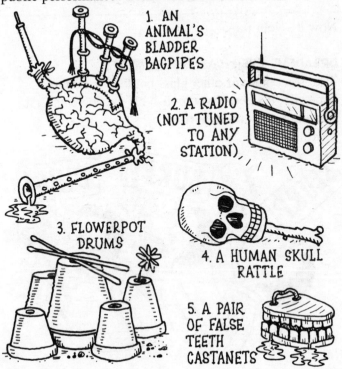

1. AN ANIMAL'S BLADDER BAGPIPES

2. A RADIO (NOT TUNED TO ANY STATION)

3. FLOWERPOT DRUMS

4. A HUMAN SKULL RATTLE

5. A PAIR OF FALSE TEETH CASTANETS

Now it's your turn…

DREADFUL EVERYDAY INSTRUMENTS

Take some milk or other glass bottles for example…
(Actually, it's best if you polish off the contents first.)

Playing a lemonade bottle

1 Drink (slurp)

Dare you discover ... how to play bottles?

You will need:
Three identical bottles
Some water
A spoon

What you do:
1 Fill a bottle with 2.5 cm of water.
2 Puff a short breath across its rim. The sound you hear is the air inside vibrating up and down.
3 Half-fill another bottle with water.
4 Puff across its rim as before.

What do you notice?
a) The sound is higher from the nearly empty bottle.
b) The sound is lower from the nearly empty bottle.
c) The sound is much louder in the half empty bottle.

Now try this...
What you do:
1 Fill the third bottle three-quarters full with water.
2 Line the bottles up in a row.
3 Tap each one with a spoon.

What do you notice?
a) The sound is higher from the nearly empty bottle.
b) The sound is lower in the nearly empty bottle.
c) When you tap the bottles water splashes everywhere.

KRAZY KAZOOS

Kazoos make an interesting if slightly weird sound.
Here's how to make your own.

You will need:
A piece of greaseproof paper
A comb

What you do:
1 Fold the greaseproof paper round the comb as shown.
2 Press your lips to the side of the kazoo as shown.
3 Here's the tricky bit. Put your lips together so they're only just open and try humming a tune. The air should be blowing out of your mouth and making the paper vibrate.
4 The wacky sound effects are made by the vibrating paper.

WARNING – Your kazoo is guaranteed to drive any adult within earshot crackers in around three seconds. Playing your kazoo while they're watching television, after bedtime, in the car or any public place can seriously damage your pocket money.

Bet you never knew!
In the 1970s one of the largest kazoos in the history of the universe was created in a factory in New York State. It was roughly the size of a door and needed five people to play it. (It's definitely a VERY SILLY idea to make your kazoo this big.)

RULER RACKETS
You will need:
One 30 cm ruler (either wood or plastic)
A table

What you do:
1 Place the ruler half on and half off the table. Hold it in place with one hand on the table.
2 Flick the free end of the ruler with your other hand.

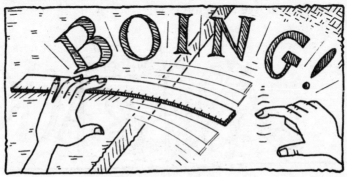

3 You can experiment with different lengths of ruler off the table to make different notes. You'll find that you hear deeper notes when more of the ruler is off the table. Yep, you got it, it's all to do with that larger area vibrating more slowly and making a lower sound.

HORRIBLE HEALTH WARNING!

Don't be tempted to play your ruler during a science lesson. Otherwise your teacher might be tempted to play the ruler, too – using you as a sounding board!

Sonic spoons

Spoons can make some brilliant sounds. The easiest way to do this is to bash two spoons together. This is best done in the privacy of your own home and not in the school canteen. Please note: I did say knock spoons together and not to knock the spoon on…

a) Any nearby priceless ornaments. This could have an effect you'll live to regret.

WHOOPS!

£9000

CRACK

b) Your teacher's head. The effects of this on you would be too painful to mention.

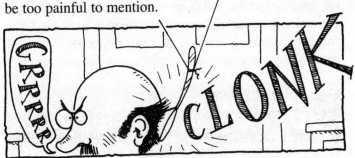

SUPER SPOON STEREO SYSTEMS

If you want to experience vibrant spoon sounds in stupendous stereo try this high-tech method. Go on, it's dreadfully awesome.

What you need:
Some string
A metal spoon

LIKE THIS!

What you do:
1 Tie some string round the metal spoon as shown.
2 Press the ends of the strings to the opening of your ear holes. Allow the spoon to bang against a tabletop. (No, I don't mean the objects in **a)** and **b)** above.) Incredible sound effect – isn't it? Solid objects like the string are very good at carrying sound waves, remember? That's why you can hear the various sounds made by the vibrating spoon amazingly well.
3 Try holding the spoon by one string whilst tapping it gently with a metal spoon. You could even try playing a tune.
4 Try experimenting with different sized spoons and metal objects such as metal colanders, egg tongs, etc.

DREADFUL SOUND EFFECTS

Of course, there's much more to sounds than making noise. How about making scary sound effects too? You could try recording them on tape to see how effective they are. Then see if your friends can guess what each one is.

A HIDEOUS SQUEAK

Rub a piece of polystyrene on a window. The squeaks you hear are actually sound waves caused as tiny lumps on the polystyrene rub quickly over bumps on the glass. Remember – don't make these noises at the wrong moment or you'll hear some hideous squeaks from your family too!

A HORRIBLE GIANT FLY

What you need:
An old cereal bag (that's the waxy bag inside a cereal packet)
A glass
A fly

What you do:

1 Catch a fly by putting a plastic glass over it. Be gentle – remember flies have feelings too.

2 Quickly put the cereal bag under the glass and gently shake the fly into it.

3 Hold the bag to your ear. The fly's footsteps and buzzing resonates in the bag and it sounds seriously dreadful.

4 After you've finished let the fly go outside. After all this is no ordinary hairy little fly – it's a hairy little sound-effect superstar.

A PHANTOM TWEET

What you need:
Half a used matchstick
40 cm of thin string
A small cottage cheese carton and lid
A pair of scissors
Sellotape

What you do:
1 Cut a 1-cm-wide hole in the side of the carton.
2 Ask for help to make a small hole in the bottom of the carton – just wide enough for the string to go through.
3 Tie one end of the string to the matchstick. Place the matchstick inside the carton and thread the string through the hole in its bottom.
4 Tape the lid in place on the carton.
5 Swing the carton on the string around your head to make a ghostly tweeting sound.

STRIKING SOUND EFFECTS

The incredible thing about the human brain is, not only can we hear sounds but we instantly know what they are. We can remember them from the first time we heard them. So you can recognize the curious choking spluttering noise made by a teacher who is just about to lose their temper and dive for cover.

If you listen to a play on the radio you will hear sound effects for things going on in the play. So how sound is your judgement? Can you match the sound effect to the way it's produced? You won't be disqualified for trying the sound effects out. Try recording them on tape and then play them back with the volume turned up.

2 A SLAP ROUND THE CHOPS

1 A GALLOPING HORSE

4 FOOTSTEPS ON A GRAVEL DRIVE

3 RAIN BEATING ON A ROOF

5 A COLLAPSING HOUSE

a) CRUSHING A WOODEN MATCHBOX

b) SCRUNCHING A BALL OF STIFF PAPER

c) SHAKING DRIED PEAS IN A BOX

d) SMACKING A HOT WATER BOTTLE

e) BEATING TWO YOGHURT POTS TOGETHER

Answers: 1 e), 2 d), 3 c), 4 b), 5 a)

If you had a go at recording those sounds, you probably won't be surprised to hear that these sound effects have all been recorded for use in radio plays. And if you want to find out more about the weird world of recorded sound, just press the button and tune in to the next chapter.

READ ON AND BE AMAZED!

ROTTEN RECORDINGS

No sound lasts for ever – it dies away as the vibrations lose energy. This is good news if the sound happens to be dreadful. No matter how rotten your school concert solo, once it's over – it's over. But thanks to the incredible invention of recorded sound your family can listen to the entire school performance full of embarrassing hiccups, raspberries and screeches over and over and over again. ARRGGGGGGHHH! So who's to blame?

Hall of fame: Thomas Edison (1847–1931)
Nationality: American
Young Thomas or Al as he was called (from Alva, his middle name) was useless at school. (Now where have we heard that before?) Al's teacher told him…

And told his mum…

Actually, what no one seemed to realize was young Al couldn't hear too well. So he couldn't hear his teachers clearly. Lucky for him, considering the cruel things they said. But it was even luckier that Al's parents were kind and understanding. They took their son away from school and taught him at home. "Luck!" I hear you say. "Sounds more like a miracle to me!"

Al loved it. He turned his dad's wood yard into a chemistry lab and burnt it down when an explosive experiment went wrong. At the age of ten he set up another chemistry lab in the basement. This was the scene for loads of dreadfully fascinating experiments that generally resulted in horrible smells, burnt clothes and wrecked furniture.

Then, at the age of 12, Al decided to get a job and started work selling newspapers and drinks on local trains. This gave him lots of time to convert the baggage carriage into a mobile chemistry lab resulting in ... you guessed it ... horrible smells, burnt clothes and wrecked furniture.

Young Al wasn't cut out to be a newspaper seller. (His destiny lay as an inventor and a scientist.) His next job was working as a telegraph clerk on his own each night.

But he found the job really tedious so he invented a machine that sent a special telegraph signal every hour to show his bosses he was still awake – while he slept. The machine worked perfectly until one night an incoming signal came in while Al was in the land of Nod. He'd hit the sack and as a result he got it – the sack that is.

For a while Al drifted from job to job. He wore scruffy clothes and rarely washed and didn't care what he ate. (Know anyone like that?) He often worked at night so he could spend the day doing scientific experiments. His big break came in New York.

He was snoozing in a friend's office because he had nowhere else to stay when the stock ticker broke. This was a kind of telegraph used to send financial information. Of course, Al was a telegraph wizard, and he fixed the machine and made it work better than before. The company bosses were so impressed that they offered Al a job.

In fact, the Western Union Telegraph Company also took an interest in the bright young man and offered him a huge contract to invent an improved telegraph. Could you achieve this kind of success? How would you measure up against the great Edison?

THOMAS EDISON QUIZ

Imagine you are Thomas A Edison. All you need to do is decide how you would act in each situation.

1 You have a technical problem with an urgent order for stock tickers. How do you solve it?

a) You lock the lab and send everyone on holiday until the problem is solved. (People have good ideas on holiday.)

b) You lock your entire staff in the lab until the problem is solved.

I'VE GOT A TECHNICAL PROBLEM WITH MY TICKER, SIR. CAN I GO HOME?

c) You lock yourself in the lab for 60 hours without food until the problem is solved.

2 You have a serious scientific problem to tackle. What do you do?

a) Call a meeting of your scientific staff and argue the question over. Make sure everyone has their say.

b) Shut yourself in a cupboard and stay there until you think of an answer.

c) Make your staff undertake dangerous experiments to prove your theories.

3 In 1871 you marry a young lady called Mary Sitwell. How do you spend your wedding day?

a) You take the week off work.

b) You go to the wedding but spend the rest of the day at the lab working on science problems.

c) You spend the whole day at the lab and ask your best man to stand in for you at the wedding.

4 You decide to improve the telephone. The acid-filled speaker invented by Alexander Graham Bell wasn't that good at picking up sounds. You look around for an alternative and discover that carbon granules are ideal for passing on the sound waves. How many substances do you test first?

a) 200 **b)** 2,000 **c)** 20,000

Answers: b) is the right answer for all the questions. Please note **2b)** is an unhealthy thing to do so don't try it.

What your answers mean.

All **bs** – congratulations you'd make a great inventor.

All **as** – you're far too laid back. Better get someone to pour you a nice cold drink while you read this book.

All **cs** – you're far too tough and too hard on everyone including yourself. Never mind – you could always become a teacher.

During the 1870s Edison made a series of brilliant inventions. After working on the telephone he became interested in the idea of storing and passing on sound waves, and in 1877 he made an unheard-of discovery.

Sounds Amazing

DOH, RAY, ME, ARGHH!

THIS WAS HIS LAST RECORDING JUST BEFORE THE ACCIDENT

TRUMPET

SOUND CYLINDER

DIAPHRAGM

NEEDLE

Flabbergast your friends with a phonograph – the latest amazing invention from Thomas A. Edison. It's really true, you *can* record and enjoy music in your own home. And guess what? Long after the singer is dead and gone, you'll still be able to hear their voice on the stunning sound cylinder!

THE SMALL PRINT
1 It's not our fault if the sound's a bit faint and scratchy.
2 Beware – the cylinder might fall apart at any moment. (That's not our fault either, OK?)

1 HOW TO RECORD YOUR OWN VOICE

SPEAK HERE

SOUND MAKES DIAPHRAGM VIBRATE

DIAPHRAGM MAKES NEEDLE VIBRATE – NEEDLE CUTS WAVY GROOVE IN CYLINDER

TURN CYLINDER

2 HOW TO LISTEN TO YOUR VOICE

SOUND WAVES FROM DIAPHRAGM PASS OUT THROUGH TRUMPET

GROOVES MAKE NEEDLE VIBRATE

TURN CYLINDER

NEEDLE MAKES DIAPHRAGM VIBRATE

321

The phonograph, as it was called, was a massive success. When one of Edison's workers took a machine to show the French Academy of Science, the scientists were so thrilled that they wanted to spend the rest of the evening playing with it.

Bet you never knew!
Amongst the weird and wacky inventions inspired by the phonograph was a talking watch made by a Mr Sivan of Geneva, Switzerland. The watch contained a tiny phonograph that called out, "WAKE UP, GET UP!" first thing in the morning. Edison himself invented a talking doll containing a phonograph that said, "Mama" or "Papa" and told stories.

Trouble was, those fragile foil cylinders really did fall apart after a couple of plays. Other inventors developed phonographs that used wax cylinders instead of foil, and then, after 1888, discs on a flat turntable. The gramophone was born.

HORRIBLE HEALTH WARNING!

Whatever you do never, never, never tamper with one of your mum's or dad's classic vinyl LPs. Grown-ups can be very strange about these dusty relics which remind them of their distant youth. A gramophone stylus needle can press down with a force of 13,608 kg per 6.5 square cm. Ignore this warning and you can expect to feel the same pressure on your head.

Of course, the march of technology has moved on dramatically since those far off prehistoric days when your parents were rather less crinkly than they are today. When you hit the big time you'll have some brilliant machines to play your latest sounds. Want to find out more?

COULD YOU BE A POP STAR? STEP 4: SERIOUS SOUND MACHINES

Once you've recorded your first single you're sure to want to listen to it again and again. And get your friends to listen to it too and even their mums and dads, pet gerbils, etc. So what sort of sound system will show you in the best possible light? Jez and Wanda are back again to help you decide.

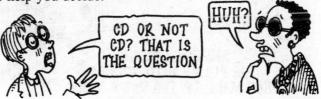

CLASSIC CASSETTE PLAYER

Jez is fiddling with this cassette recorder. This machine turns sound into magnetic signals and back again. Sounds incredible, doesn't it?

SOUND CAUSES THE RECORDING HEAD TO MAKE A MAGNETIC SIGNAL

WOOF!

MIKE PICKS UP SOUND WAVES

THE SIGNAL MAKES A PATTERN OF MAGNETIC BITS ON THE TAPE

And now Wanda's going to demonstrate what happens when you play a tape.

MAGNETIC BITS ON THE TAPE HEAD FIRE ELECTRICAL PULSES

WOOF!

AMPLIFIER TURNS THE PULSES INTO SOUNDS THAT MAKE UP THE DOG'S WOOF

Jez and Wanda are investigating a CD player. A CD stores sounds as tiny pits on its surface. The CD player turns these into electrical signals … here's what happens.

325

When Jez plays the CD disc it spins round mega fast…
And here's where it gets really technical…

Look inside the CD player and you'll find how to turn the pulses back into sounds.

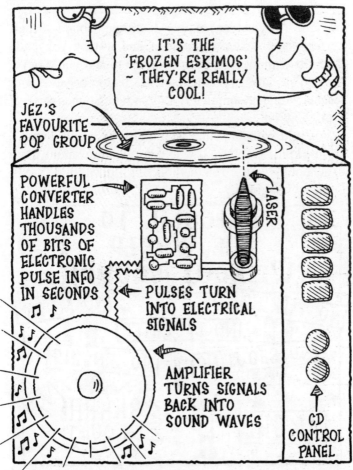

IT'S THE 'FROZEN ESKIMOS' ~ THEY'RE REALLY COOL!

JEZ'S FAVOURITE POP GROUP

POWERFUL CONVERTER HANDLES THOUSANDS OF BITS OF ELECTRONIC PULSE INFO IN SECONDS

LASER

PULSES TURN INTO ELECTRICAL SIGNALS

AMPLIFIER TURNS SIGNALS BACK INTO SOUND WAVES

CD CONTROL PANEL

If it all works the CD player produces better sound quality than the tape. Tapes can get twisted or dirty which spoils the sound quality. But the laser beam only picks up the pits on the CD rather than any bits of grease or fluff on its surface.

SOUNDING IT OUT

Imagine (if you can) a world without sound. Peace, perfect peace – silence is golden, and all that. You could doze off without ever being woken up, and you'd never have to sit through another science lesson because your teacher would be completely tongue-tied. Sounds perfect? Well, hold on…

A world without sound would also be a dull, lifeless, joyless kind of a place. It would be a bit like having to go to school by yourself in the holidays – only far WORSE. Can you imagine it?

There'd be no games of football (can you imagine a totally quiet game?), no chatting on the phone, no one telling jokes, and definitely NO rude noises. There'd be NO FUN. Nothing but a vast horribly gloomy silence. Sounds dreadful. Could you bear it?

OK, you can turn the volume up again now, and appreciate some of the good sounds you can tune into…

And every year brings sensational sound discoveries… Time was when the most thrilling sound experience you could look forward to was listening to your grandad tinkling a dodgy old piano and singing awful old songs. Nowadays you can listen to whatever you want, whenever you want, and you can pick up a phone and natter to people on the other side of the world.

BUT SOUND SCIENCE DISCOVERIES AREN'T JUST FOR FUN…

At this very minute scientists are working on new and incredible sound discoveries. Discoveries that will make it easier for people to keep in contact and find out new information. Here are a few that we're already using…

SUPERSONIC SOUND SIGNALS

• Optical fibres send signals as pulses of light to be made into sounds by a phone. So your voice can be turned into an incredible flashing light code. It's then turned back into sound waves so the person on the other end of the phone can understand you.

• Video phones transmit not only the sound of your voice but also live pictures of you talking. (This could be embarrassing if someone called when you were on the toilet.)

• A computer can actually chat to you. Here's how…

1 Someone speaks words into a machine that turns sound into electronic pulses.

2 These pulses are stored as codes in the computer's vast memory.

3 When the computer speaks the codes are turned back into pulses.

4 And these are converted into sounds which come out of the computer's speakers.

And sounds can even make people *healthier.*

STUNNING SURGICAL SOUND SYSTEMS

• Ultrasound pulses blast kidney stones. The vibrations break up the painful stones but don't harm the wobbly flesh that surrounds them. Pow!

• Ultrasound scans can produce SONAR-style pictures of unborn babies inside their mums. The picture can be used to check that the babies are OK.

EVERYTHING'S FINE, SHE'S GIVING US THE THUMBS UP!

Sometimes science seems boring, and at times the boring bits can sound really dreadful. But outside the classroom there's a great big world bursting with sound. A huge exciting vibrant world alive with loud, shocking, shrieking, spectacular noises, and thanks to science it's getting more amazing all the time.

The future sounds dreadfully exciting, doesn't it?

SOUNDS DREADFUL

DREADFUL

QUIZ

Now find out if you're a
Sounds Dreadful expert!

So – reckon you've understood ears and sussed out sound? Take these quick quizzes and find out whether you've really been listening carefully or whether these words have fallen on deaf ears...

Horrible human sounds

Humans are among the nastiest, noisiest creatures in the animal kingdom. We might not be able to hear as well as other animals, but we can distinguish between thousands of different sounds – and, boy, can we make a racket...

1 In which part of the ear are the ear bones found?
a) Middle ear
b) Inner ear
c) Ear drum

2 Which of the following can cause deafness?
a) Listening to birdsong.
b) Listening to loud music.
c) Listening to your science teacher droning on.

3 What hideous human sound is made by air escaping from the stomach?
a) A fart
b) A burp
c) A whistle

4 What is the fluid in your ears' semi-circular canals for?
a) It helps you balance.
b) It makes you sneeze.
c) It picks up sound vibrations.

5 What is a cochlea implant?
a) An ear trumpet made of brass to help the hard of hearing.
b) A flap of skin added to the ear lobe to help the hard of hearing.
c) A tiny radio receiver placed under the skin to help the hard of hearing.

6 What is the more common name for cerumen?
a) Ear lobe
b) Ear wax
c) Snot

7 What would a conversation be like in space?
a) Slower – it takes sound waves longer to pass through a vacuum.
b) Faster – sound waves travel more quickly through a vacuum.
c) Nothing – sound waves can't travel through a vacuum.

8 What horrible body noise is made by a vibrating uvula?
a) A snore
b) A humming in your head
c) A fart

Answers:
1a; 2b; 3b; 4a; 5c; 6b; 7c; 8a

Super sound waves

Sound is a bit like the sea – OK, it's not wet and full of fish but it does come in waves. So are you wired up to making sense of those weird waves of sound?

1 Which part of the ear vibrates when sound waves hit it? (Clue: Your teacher might *beat* it out of you!)

2 What unit is used for measuring sound? (Clue: 10 bells?)

3 What sound is heard when sound waves hit a solid surface? (Clue: What sound is heard when sound waves hit a solid surface?)

4 Where do the vibrations that cause humming originate? (Clue: Come on – you *nose*…)

5 What noise do you hear when you break the sound barrier? (Clue: sounds like Chronic Doom)

6 What carries sound signals to the brain? (Clue: You might be shaking with these)

7 What sound technology was used to try and find the Loch Ness Monster? (Clue: ...and yet *so far*)

8 What amazing machine did Alexander Graham Bell invent to carry sound waves thousands of kilometres? (Clue: It was a good call)

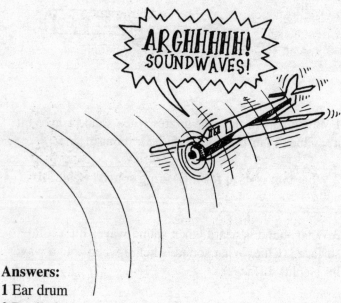

Answers:
1 Ear drum
2 Decibels
3 Echo
4 Nostrils
5 Sonic boom
6 Nerves
7 SONAR
8 Telephone

Strange sound sayings

The science of sound is filled with strange vocabulary. Have you been listening carefully enough to match the following weird words with their deafening definitions?

1 Frequency
2 Oscilloscope
3 Resonance
4 Acoustics

5 Amplitude
6 Ultrasound
7 Tone
8 Harmonics

a) A group of different tones.
b) A sound with just one frequency.
c) Sound above the range of human hearing.
d) The number of vibrations a second that make up a sound.
e) A machine for measuring sound waves.
f) Sound vibrations at a certain frequency.
g) The science of sound production, transmission and effects.
h) How loud a sound is.

Answers:
1d; 2e; 3f; 4g; 5h; 6c; 7b; 8a

Strange sound facts

Scientists have made many amazing discoveries about sound and how it works. Some are almost unbelievable. And some perhaps shouldn't be believed... Can you tell the fact from the fiction among these strange sound facts?

1 Sound travels much more quickly through air than it does through metal.

2 Sound waves can knock holes in solid objects.

3 The variety of sounds a human can make is fewer than those of other mammals.

4 The sound you hear when you crack your knuckles is just a load of old gas.

5 Each of your ears hears sounds of slightly different pitches.

6 If you put a seashell to your ear the sound you hear is the sound of your own blood moving through your body.

7 Snores can be as loud as a pneumatic drill.

8 A whip makes a cracking sound because its tip moves faster than the speed of sound.

Answers:

1 FALSE. Sound travels 15 times faster through steel than it does through air!

2 TRUE. A machine built by NASA could make 210 decibels of sound – and could damage more than just ear drums...

3 FALSE. Humans can make many more different sounds than other animals because their tongues and lips can move in so many different ways.

4 TRUE. It's the sound of nitrogen gas bubbles bursting.

5 TRUE. The right ear often hears higher noises than the left.

6 FALSE. Sorry, it's just the boring old sounds around you resonating in the shell. It works just as well with your granny's tea cup – just make sure it's empty first.

7 TRUE. Snores have been known to reach over 90 decibels – as loud as a drill and loud enough to cause damage to your ears!

8 TRUE. It's a *striking* sonic boom!

Amazing animal noises

You might know what it means when your cat purrs or your dog barks, but animals have many amazingly complicated ways of saying different things. Can you recognize these cunning creatures just by the sound of their voices?

1 My voice sounds like a series of curious clicks, but I don't use vocal chords – I just pass air through air sacs in my head!

2 I stand a much better chance of romancing a lady because vibrating air-filled pouches in my croaking throat make my song of luurrve even louder.

3 I make a s-s-special s-s-sound by vibrating pieces of bone in my tail to warn that I'm in a bad mood.

4 I just rub my legs together, and hey presto, a cacophony of sound shimmers through the quiet evening as I chat with my friends.

5 My eyesight is poor so I emit tiny squeaks – too high for you humans to hear – to find my way around.

6 My moods aren't hard to spot – I will purr, grunt, moan, growl and snarl. But my scariest sound can carry for kilometres across the savannah…

7 I can get a message to a mate more than 800 km away. My strange song starts in my throat and moves to a bag linked to my nose!

8 My ears have a wide range of motion, so I can hear sounds up to 16 km away – and I'll react to them by throwing back my head and making my own distinctive sound in the moonlight…

a) Whale
b) Bat
c) Dolphin
d) Grasshopper
e) Rattlesnake
f) Wolf
g) Frog
h) Lion

Answers:
1c; 2g; 3e; 4d; 5b; 6h; 7a; 8f

HORRIBLE INDEX

aardvarks 247
acoustics 252–3
aerophones 296
aeroplanes 224–9
air pressure 192
alpine horns 251
amplifiers 186, 201, 238, 295, 303, 324, 327
amplitude (loudness) 181, 213, 233, 255
anvil (ear bone) 195
Auenbrugg, Leopold (Austrian doctor) 267
ausculation (listening to body) 268–9
avalanches 192

babies, bawling 177, 235, 330
balancing, how to 194
Ballot, Christoph Buys (Dutch scientist) 219–20
bang, biggest 234
bass, double 215, 294
bats, biting 181, 193, 247, 254–8
Baudelaire, Charles (French poet) 288
Beethoven, Ludwig van (German composer) 202–5
Bell, Alexander Graham (British-American inventor) 233, 277–80, 282–5, 320
bells 179, 212, 277, 280, 283
birds 189–90, 202, 242, 244, 248
blood vessels, bursting 179, 212
bones 193–5, 205, 211, 301
booms, sonic 229–31

bottles, playing 306–8
brain 194, 196, 198–9, 201, 247, 286, 314
brass instruments 296, 300
breathing 191, 218, 249, 265, 269, 290, 307
bronchitis (dire disease) 270
burping 264, 266

Cage, John (American composer) 306
canals, semi-circular 194, 196
cassette recorders 324
CDs 323, 325–7
cetaceans (whales/dolphins) 248
Charles II (British king) 275–6
chat lines, launched 283
chimps, cheeky 243
chordophones 296
cicadas, crazy 244
clapping 212
cochlea, spiral-shaped 194, 196, 200–1, 233
concert halls, planning 251–4
crickets, cranky 246–7
Cromwell, Oliver (British roundhead ruler) 275–6
crystals, chemical 201
currents 187, 281

deafness 182, 200–11, 236, 278
death 224–8, 237
decibels (dB) 232–3, 235–6, 244, 248, 265, 274
Deutsch, Diana (American scientist) 199

diaphragms, thin 186, 222, 281, 321
DJs 184
dolphins 248–9, 255, 258
Doppler, Christian (Austrian scientist) 219–20
Doppler effect 219–20
drums 296, 301–2
drumsticks 205, 302

eardrums 192, 194–5, 218, 233, 247
earmuffs 236, 290
earphones 293
earplugs 231, 304
ears 193–211, 214, 218, 224, 245–8, 258
echoes, eerie 249–63, 304
Edison, Thomas (American inventor) 316–22
egg boxes, extremely useful 185, 240
electric instruments 295
electrons (tiny energy bits) 213
elephants 246–7, 258, 272

factories, foul tempers in 236
farting, foul 264–5, 272
fingernails, down blackboard 235
foghorns 251
forks, tuning 182
frequency, fantastic 181–2, 197, 213–5, 245, 255, 292, 308
frogs 188, 190, 241, 246–7

galleries, whispering 250
glass 179, 227, 288, 292
gramophones 322–3
grasshoppers 193, 245, 247
Gray, Elisha (American inventor) 280, 282–4
guitars, groovy 183, 239, 294–5
guns 179, 221–2, 237

hammer (ear bone) 195

hands, tapping on 208–9, 268
harmonics 183
hearing 193–211, 224, 317
hearing aids, helpful 201–2
heartbeat 221, 269–70
Hendrix, Jimi (American guitar wizard) 239
Hertz (Hz) 181, 199, 214, 245, 291
high-frequency sounds 214–5, 219–20, 235
high-pitched sounds 188–90, 213, 245, 247, 273
humming 266, 272, 308

idiophones 296
infrasound (too low to hear) 237
inner ear 193–4, 205, 233
insulators 184
interference, destructive 254

jaws 271, 279
Jurinne, Charles (Swiss scientist) 254

kazoos 308–9
Keller, Helen (American heroine) 206–10
Krakatau (Krakatoa) 234

Laénnec, René (French doctor) 269–70
Langevin, Paul (French scientist) 258–9
larynx (throat bit) 271
lava (liquid rock) 234
left ear 199
light 221, 231, 250, 329
lightning 229–31
lips 271, 273, 279
listening 191, 200, 217, 238, 269, 287, 321
loudspeakers 186–8, 285
low-frequency sounds 215, 219, 247, 308
low-pitched sounds 188, 213, 246, 251

McAdams, Steve (Canadian scientist) 198
Mach 1 (speed of sound) 224
Mach, Ernst (Austrian scientist) 223–4
megaphones 275–7
melodies, making 202
membranophones 296
Mersenne, Marin (French priest/ scientist) 221
microphones 185–7, 201
middle ear 194–5, 200, 202
mixing 303–4
monkeys, howling 243
Morita, Akiro (Japanese inventor) 325
Morland, Samuel (British inventor) 275–6
moths 246–7, 255–7
Mozart, Wolfgang A (Austrian composer) 287
mp3 players 325
music 200–2, 204, 218
    broadcasting 285
    indoors 251–4
    mayhem with 286–304, 328–9
    recording 316–27
    as weapon 238–9
musical instruments 197–8, 293–315
musicians 287, 289

nature, noisy 241–9
needles, in groove 321, 323
nerves 194, 196, 198–201, 286
Nessie (Loch Ness monster) 259–63
noises, nuisance 177–8, 235, 312–4
Noriega, General (Panamanian leader) 237–40
noses, bleeding 212

oscilloscopes (measure sound waves) 213
owls 246–7

peaks 213
percussion 296, 301–3
phonographs 321–2
pianos 204–5, 245, 291, 296–8, 303, 329
pitch 188–90, 213, 219, 245–7, 251, 273, 291–2
producers 184
pulses 186, 201, 248, 259, 281, 324, 326–7, 329–30
pus 200

rackets, infernal 236, 245, 309–10
radio 201, 305–6, 314–5
raspberries, blowing 264
rats, rowdy 242
recording, rotten 303–4, 316–27
Regnault, Henri (French scientist) 222
resonance, rumbling 182, 291–3, 295, 313
right ear 199
Rossini, GS (Italian composer) 288
rubber bands, twanging 205, 216, 218
rulers, playing 309–10

samplers 303–4
satellite dishes, faces like 247
saxophones 298–9
shouting 274–5
signals, super 194, 196, 198–9, 201, 281, 295, 303, 318, 324–5, 327, 329
singing 242, 289–93, 321, 328–9
skulls 205, 271, 305–6
snakes 189–90, 246–7
snoring 265
SONAR (SOund NAvigation and Ranging) 258, 260, 262–3, 330
sound barrier, breaking 225–6, 228–9
sound effects 305–15
soundproofing 184–5, 240, 293
space, no good screaming in 213

speed of sound, faster than 221–8
spoons, playing 310–11
stars, pop 183–8, 289–93, 323
stereo 240, 311
stethoscopes 269–70
stirrup (ear bone) 195
stridulation (leg-rubbing) 245
stringed instruments 294–6
supersonic (faster than sound)
220–31, 329–30
synthesizers 302
syrinxes, singing 242

talking 199, 203, 207, 272–9
tapes 324, 327
telephones 281–5, 320, 328–30
thunder 229–31, 251
timbre 198
tones, tuneful 181–3
tongue 271, 273, 279
transducers 258–9
transistors 187
transmitters 201, 281
trumpets 201–2, 300, 305, 321
turbulence, terrifying 211, 228
Twain, Mark (American novelist) 288
tweeters 187–8, 313–4

ultrasound (too high to hear) 242,
249, 255, 330
uvula (dangling throat bit) 265

vesicles, activating 257
vibrations 178, 181–3, 186–7, 197
    in abdomen 244
    in ears 193–4, 201, 205, 211
    in eyeballs 292
    giant 229
    on ground 247
    in gullet 266
    in instruments 295, 299,
307–8, 310–11
    in intestines 237
    in kettles 301
    losing 185, 316

measuring 213
    in mouth 266, 273
    muffling 218
    in music 291–2
    per second 181, 214–5, 218
    putting teeth on edge 235
    recording 321
    singing 289
    on skin 247, 265–6
    in telephones 281
    in throat 209, 273
    whistling 242
video phones 330
vinyl 323
violins 215, 294, 296
vocal chords 215, 271, 273, 289
voices 215–7, 271, 273, 278, 321,
329
volcanoes, violent 234
Wagner, Richard (German
composer) 288
Walkman, Sony 325
Watson, Thomas (Bell's assistant)
280, 282–3
waves
    bouncing 250, 252–3, 258
    cancelled out 254
    carrying 311
    changing direction 224
    finding things 258–9
    from flashing lights 330
    helping with tests 287
    in instruments 303
    long 246
    making holes 236
    in music 292
    recording 321, 324, 327
    seeing 216–7
    shock 234
    in skull 271
    soaking up 240, 253
    speedy 212–31
    squashed 219
    storing 320
    in telephones 281

347

tidal 234
    as weapons 237–9
waves in water 192, 201, 211, 217–8
wax 194–5, 321–2
weapons, deadly 237–9
whales 248–9, 258
whispering 250, 271
whistling 242, 266, 274

wind instruments 301
windows, oval 193–4
woodpeckers, wonderful 244
woodwind instruments 296, 298–9
woofers 187–8

Yeager, Chuck (American pilot) 225–9

Nick Arnold has been writing stories and books since he was a youngster, but never dreamt he'd find fame writing about dreadful sound. His research involved singing in the bath, shouting at the top of his voice and trying to decipher the lyrics to pop songs and he enjoyed every minute of it.

When he's not delving into Horrible Science, he spends his spare time eating pizza, riding his bike and thinking up corny jokes (though not all at the same time).

Tony De Saulles picked up his crayons when he was still in nappies and has been doodling ever since. He takes Horrible Science very seriously and even agreed to investigate if snakes have ears. Fortunately, his injuries weren't too serious.

When he's not out with his sketchpad, Tony likes to write poetry and play squash, though he hasn't written any poetry about squash yet.

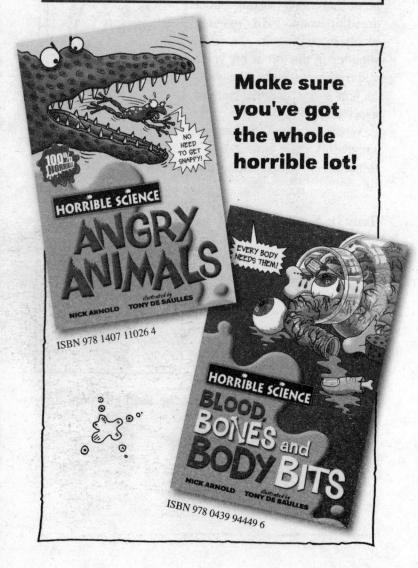